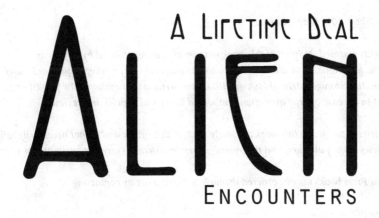

A LIFETIME DEAL

ALIEN

ENCOUNTERS

JUDY L. CLARKE

BALBOA.
PRESS
A DIVISION OF HAY HOUSE

Balboa Press books may be ordered through booksellers or by contacting:

Balboa Press
A Division of Hay House
1663 Liberty Drive
Bloomington, IN 47403
www.balboapress.com.au
1-(877) 407-4847

Printed in the United States of America

ISBN: 978-1-4525-0200-7 (sc)
ISBN: 978-1-4525-0201-4 (e)

Balboa Press rev. date: 05/12/2011

Legend

Dedication

This book is dedicated to my mother, Daphne Schroder (born 18 November, 1923) for her steadfast love, understanding, support, and never-ending faith in everything I have ever done. I openly declare my love and adoration to a woman who dedicated her life to her husband and daughters. She did more for others than she ever did for herself. I couldn't have hand picked a better mother, friend, or neighbour. To the best mother in the world, I love you.

Acknowledgements

Many grateful thanks to all the wonderful people from this world who have supported and unconditionally stood by me through all my trials and tribulations in this life of mine, specifically, Donna Campbell, Geraldine Mutton, Judy Moon, Earl Smith, Christina Stuart, Michelle Robertson, and Liz Howe-Sloane (long-term friendships that have stood the test of time). Vicki Woodage (editor-in-training—grateful thanks). Not to mention, my constant book-writing companion who was right beside me every step of the way—Angel, my Shih Tzu Dog.

In addition, a heartfelt thanks and appreciation to all those wonderful "beings" not of this world that have subconsciously educated me throughout my life, listened to my thoughts and prayers, and guided me in the direction of best outcomes for the good of all.

Finally, for pushing my lessons under my nose and forcing me to cherish choice, because there is always a choice of doors waiting to be opened, and that choice is ours alone. Regardless of how much pain and discomfort I have endured to reach the goals in my life—some of which are still unclear—I shall always strive to reach the highest pinnacle that I am able to with your never-ending guidance, presence, and love.

I thank you with all that I am.

Judy Clarke

TESTIMONIALS

"Like so many other closet believers in UFOs and the entities that control them, I am hungry for credible information that further reinforces our beliefs to a level where we can openly (without fear of ridicule) discuss these issues. Once again, I admire Judy greatly for having the strength of her convictions to further educate the rest of us by recounting her own personal experiences in this area. I found her book captivating."

Earl D. Smith, Master 4 Res. M.E.D. Grade 1

"A gentle and reasonable approach. To the point and thought-provoking. Well-done."

Geraldine Mutton

"Your book, from the outset, is really very engaging. It tugs away at our basic human fears and immediately grabs our attention. Alien abductions are an old story, but it is a subject we never tire of, because we are both scared and fascinated at the same time. This book is a great basis for one of those 'change your life' books. Admittedly, there will be the usual skeptics, who will immediately discount your writing as the sheer 'rantings' of a madwoman, but you will strike a chord in those individuals who have a deeper sense of spiritual purpose, whether they are religiously inclined or not. This book is just *brilliant!* It captivated me from start to finish. Your voice resonates strongly in this piece, and your words have so much impact. It has left a lasting impression on me—a desire to read more of your writing. It is also very *powerful.* Wow, I think I am speechless, and that is saying something."

Emily Lannan, RN

"I can see this book as a Spielberg movie, capturing all the chapters with the intensity it was written. It is sensible and opens people's eyes about what is going on. I've turned from a skeptic to a believer. You are a wonderful and gifted writer with a very descriptive style. I am proud of you."

Daphne Schroder

"Judy has shown great courage in the undertaking and writing of this book. The subject about alien abduction is very controversial and challenging to a readership that has little or no knowledge about such matters. Most people would shy away from such a bizarre subject, because it is literally mind-boggling. Judy, however, has wrestled with this experience from a very young age and spent the rest of her life trying to make sense of it. Now, with excellent helmsmanship in her writing style, the truth about her personal journey is finally being expressed. Her story will no doubt open a floodgate of serious questions as well as cause a huge swell of negative flack from those whose lives are strictly limited to the safe and familiar reality. This book is a book that had to be written *now.* A truly fascinating read and a timely reminder of who we are—travellers in time! I wish Judy well in this endeavor as I believe her to be quite a remarkable human being."

Judy Moon RN, Dip. Yoga, BA.N, Dip. Mid.

PROLOGUE

Judy's intention is to take the fear factor out of alien abduction putting the reader, who feels they may have had this experience, more at ease, while explaining her journey over decades of coincidences and occurrences. She has carefully compiled a lifetime of memories and experiences that have slowly revealed themselves to enable the revelation of the bigger picture of what *is* and what could be happening. This is written in a chapter-by-chapter compilation from infancy, approximately every two years over the span of her life. These alien encounters have followed her through changes of address, travelling around the world and living overseas, and then returning back home again in more recent times.

Once visitation is established, this seems to be an ongoing occurrence. As far as can be established, quite often, abduction is an inherited occurrence and goes from parent(s) to child(ren), but not in all cases. Judy is unsure of her parental involvement in alien abduction, but wants it known that we can be in ignorance all our lives of encounters such as these. This subject was very seldom discussed with friends or family, brought about by an ambivalent complacency—a feeling of unimportance to even raise the subject. Although she believes there may be alien involvement with her son, this subject has never been broached.

Judy explains her lack of fear with her captors, the language used for perfect communication, while giving the reader a panoramic and descriptive vista as she takes them through her experiences, describing both the inside of the spacecraft and the aliens themselves while taking into account their personality and characters. She gives a visual, step-by-step account of the transfer from her bed to boarding the UFO and back again. Judy goes on to explain to the best of her ability her view of why this is occurring and concludes with her own assumptions and advice for the future. It's not a scary story, but an enlightening one—one that allows an individual to realise there isn't anything scary in the world unless we allow it to be. It all began in 1952 and continues to today.

Introduction

In the beginning, God created the heavens and the earth—this means everything in the universe, *everything*. Carry that sentence with you as we move on.

My journey began in this life on our wonderful planet called Earth in 1951. Shortly after, through a serious health issue, I ended up in hospital. This journey—my journey—begins at this point, in the Auckland hospital in New Zealand. Apparently, a number of other children in the Auckland region were also hospitalised with this very same issue, as it swept across the Auckland region in a notable wave on the map. This ended up being the beginning of a lifetime of alien abductions. While remaining compliant to a contract, a lifetime deal had been arranged before my birth, with no present memory of it until now.

House moves only went to prove that no matter where you live in the world, if you are on the list, you will be found. After-effects, like skin marks, bruises, and waking up early enough to often times having remnants of memory (or in one case, pain), I knew I wasn't altogether alone, and no matter what, I always awoke back in my bed, with no memory of being taken.

We have all experienced "coincidences," but how many of us, I wonder, have had countless coincidences, leading to life-saving events—especially when there have been telepathic warnings to bring about evasive action?

My life is cram-packed with experiences and confirmations, and within these pages, I will be leading you through my life. Keep in mind, we are always returned unharmed, except for what we singlehandedly do to ourselves in the name of fear—all the same, we are returned.

Appearing on "A Current Affair" along with Budd Hopkins (a famous UFO investigator) was a nerve-wracking experience, more so just for virtue of being on national television, proving there are some abductees who come from a fearful space and others who do not. Life has a way of leading us to where we are meant to be, regardless of our intentions. Although, of course, we do have "free will" and "spontaneity," and most times, our dreams of our futures are planned along with God's ideas for us. The power of positive thought or prayer attracts that which you desire, as you will see. With me, I said a prayer for a Bible—a book I'd never read before—to decipher a dream; then out of the blue, four arrived in one day. That's what I call a prayer being answered. This brings me to the present day, with a few more answers than when I started. Happy reading.

CHAPTER ONE

What It's All About

Sometimes I wonder what stimulates us do things and to what lengths we go to finally push us to the point of stepping up to the plate when we could have done so years before and didn't. Why do we do things and leave the memory of them in the back of our minds? Is it we who forget, or is that memory lapse induced by outside sources? Knowing full well those things were real, we won't allow the accumulation of those memories to join together to make the story they truly are come to life, like a selective memory.

A series of events occurred in my life that seemed to open the floodgates for the release of some haunting memories of alien encounters that happened at various times throughout my life, bringing small prompters back to me. These prompters ranged from straight-up recall, to hypnotism, to seeing a book jacket, to pictures, to casual conversations, to movies, to waking up just knowing, etc. Even when these memories came to mind, they were not something I felt drawn to talk about. I owned a complacency—a "couldn't care less" (cavalier) attitude, a plain and simple lack of desire to discuss it—which was very strange for me, as I'm never short of a word. Then again, one has to think, *Was this an inflicted silence to prevent talk on a subject that must be kept quiet until the time was right?* Were, in fact, all abductees given this same enforced silence until we were given permission to open up and talk about it? It makes me think that maybe now is the time.

Throughout my life, intermittent memories and disjointed visions came to mind, confirming that I had seen and had been in the company of little people (greys), not of this world. They looked like little children in silver suits and stood about three to four feet tall (the same size as a child). Of the people who claim to have been abducted, the multitude have a resultant fear, anger, or disbelief, showing itself in nightmares, pre-sleep stress, insomnia, and anger, and sometimes even in psychological illness or paranoia.

My memory was given a huge wakeup call following the release of the book *Communion* way back in the 80s, and from that point onward, the flood gates to some of my past memories began to surface from many years before, and many questions I had never asked began to become more important to me. The book *Communion* cannot be blamed for dreaming my experiences up, nor for me imagining that I was experiencing the same things as Whitley Streiber claimed within his book from his abductions. Mine were nothing like his. Strieber's abductions began from adulthood, so he believes, and affected him badly, whereas mine began from infancy (nine months of age). Maybe this is why I was not so fearful, due to growing up with them.

I had become acclimatized subconsciously to them, in the absence of fear, understanding their silent language and apparently loving them enough to want to remain with them instead of returning home to be with my own family here on earth. Force was not necessary with a child who responded well to them.

Adult abductees are right out of their comfort zones, suddenly being in a place they don't recognize, being transported in a way that is picture perfect out of a nightmare, rendering them paralyzed yet open-eyed and awake to see and experience their surroundings while being unable to move. This is the stuff that nightmares are made of. No doubt fearfulness in the extreme would grasp any victim of such an event, offering nothing but snippets of memory that result in dreams, because nothing like this could possibly happen in reality.

Any amount of attempts by aliens to communicate with humans by telepathic means (their only means of communication) amidst fear are usually not recognised. Things like our inner chatter, screaming, demands to be let go, and struggling and fighting to gain freedom all go to block the chances of incoming telepathic communication, rendering a non-established link. With this in mind, these little grey aliens appear to be silent, emotionless, cruel, and non-caring individuals who only want to hurt and inflict injury—which, of course, is untrue. We have heard the odd, scary testimonials from the public, but sadly, very seldom do we hear reports of friendship, kindness, and a reluctance to want to return home. Usually a complete denial exists from our governments and armed forces, offering the world a whitewashed excuse that aliens do not exist and anyone stating they have seen them is lying, imagining things, or needs incarcerating (which has been done). Even today, the USA is telling us there is no one out there in our big, vast universe but us, otherwise they would know about it. The thing is, they do know about it.

Our age is as irrelevant to them as time is; it makes no difference. Where education and explanations are concerned, even a small child can receive uncontaminated incoming information with education far exceeding normal scholarly standards. Their teaching of knowledge is not linear, as ours is, with sentence after sentence and word after word so that only some of the intended knowledge is imparted, received, heard, and understood with a mind and memory that have to collate it all together to make sense of it. Telepathy is a holistic thought process, allowing no misconstrued messages or mistakes; they are words, visions, feelings, thoughts—a complete and utter, all-encompassing knowledge, without misperceptions. This is transferred to the recipient, offering the same incoming messages as scientists would seek out following their graduating degrees, diplomas, and scholarly achievements. Infants and children have the same incoming data as adults. The concept of this is so out of human concept that it is difficult to explain. When mind communicates with mind, there is a 100 percent non-fail communication with no room for mistakes of any kind.

Now, when I look into the night sky, a part of me remembers how it used to be, but can't work out the why or how. The star patterns, planetary positions, and pathways travelled are no longer clear. When ETs are in our skies, I can sense their presence—that could be put down to me picking up their telepathy. Nothing takes away the intense attraction to the night sky and the longing to see movement or proof that someone is out there.

I have been the recipient of invasive sampling and insertions of physical and ethereal implants. These can be from nearly any part of the body—for example, the nose, mouth, vagina, rectum, ear, and skin, along with implantation areas into bone, behind the eye, the brain, the ear, nose and skin. Some implants are automatically rejected at certain times, like a battery winding down and no longer working, or they are autolyzed by the body; some have to be removed at future visits, and some are replaced.

I have to admit, only on one occasion did I awake in severe pain, but I shall go into that later in the book. At all other times, there was no hint of discomfort or memory. Such things that a baby or child cannot consent to baffled me as I got older, because consent is a given, universal understanding (something I feel to be true). This consent had to have been obtained prior to my birth—which I found out later began many lifetimes ago.

While living, all memories prior to our births evade us, and most contracts with them are agreed upon prior to birth and continue each time we are born, giving permission for a lifetime of abductions. Due to lack of memory, we imagine they are doing something to us we haven't agreed upon—but we have; we just don't remember it.

Upon waking, each time I was taken, it was as if I had simply woken from my night's sleep, with the memory of each abduction being erased to the point of absolute ignorance—although on occasion, I was left with marks or bruising on various areas of my body, some of which are still evident today, proving that my sleep times were not altogether spent in slumber. Something had to have occurred that I didn't understand or believe. In most cases, I was oblivious to how those marks got there. My parents were certainly ignorant to the fact that abductions went on, let alone to their own daughter. If I would have questioned them on the idea of UFOs or aliens, I would have been adopted out in disgust or given away to the orphanage down the road (a common threat if I misbehaved). Not even the medical profession was able to explain away how the marks arrived on my leg from my stay in hospital.

What puzzles me now is that I didn't seem to question or worry about any of it at all as I was growing up. I accepted the explanation my parent gave me—that it was caused by injections from my stay in hospital as a baby. It is only in latter years I remembered how this mark got to be there, as scene by scene played out, until the realization came that this mark was made during an alien encounter. This answered all my questions regarding the ominous marks on my leg.

My parents gave me an explanation that kept my inquisitive mind from investigating until later in life, when I became a nurse. I then realised that the explanation I swallowed was utter rubbish. This is when my search began.

When the book *Communion* was released back in the 1980s, I'd never heard of Whitley Streiber. There has always been an internalized instinct—a feeling that UFOs were a reality out there in the cosmos. Even as a small child, I believed there would have to be. If UFOs had been seen and reported by so many people worldwide, then there had to be a whom or a what to fly them. I had a very strong faith (in the absence of any proof) that they existed, regardless of what the multitudes believed or what any government professed to say (propaganda) or explain away. I knew—and that, to me, was rock solid. Sometimes we have to be true to ourselves, regardless of what others may say or believe.

We, the human race, are children, overstepping the boundaries of caretaking a planet that we are fast destroying. Does mother nature take care of herself, or are there greater governing bodies that we don't know about?

Movies released over the last several decades are introducing us all to the idea of alien invasion, other planets, landings, and sightings, even to the point of earth's destruction or doomsday events. Some of these movies show us the possibility of life on other planets. Not all life is the same in looks, temperament, communication, and abilities.

I stopped myself writing on this subject several years ago, because the human race wasn't ready to hear what has been going on all around us for centuries. Who wants to believe or understand about other worldly beings, their crashes, their reasons for coming here, and our involvement—especially when the government and the paparazzi point the fingers at these victims with laughter, ridicule, disbelief, and horror? Who wants to appear crazy or insane to the rest of the world? And who has the courage—especially those with a professional, credible background—to take the chance of being discredited to the point of losing one's job, income, respect, and life, for that matter? Well, it seems I do. In most cases, an enforced loss of memory prevents the truth from being told.

I will be talking about the coincidences and chain of events that have lead me to believe that for whatever reason, I am being guided along a spiritual path. It may be to show others that forgiveness, kindness, empathy, and understanding are the way to go; it may be to touch people's lives gently and then move on. It may be to experience what I know to be the truth and allow others to learn by my openness about it, or simply to write this book to eradicate the fear that surrounds the terms *UFO* and *aliens* and allow some type of preparation for their eventual arrival. I have noticed that other abductees are beginning to meet up, talk about it, reveal their experiences, and—wonder of wonders—we all are realising that we all basically have similar stories, knowledge, and temperaments.

Chapter Two

Hospital Visit in New Zealand—
Nine Months of Age

It all began when I was a mere babe in arms—only nine months old and not walking yet. For some time, I was progressively worsening, with a kidney problem that (even by today's standards) was a threat to my life. This illness originated from a common bacterial strain known as streptococcus (strep). What started out in the throat ended up by compromising the functioning ability of my kidneys, to the point of my coming very close to death.

Apparently, I was amongst a cluster of infants and young children affected with Nephritis in Auckland, New Zealand back in 1952.

It was in 1952 that Dr. Alice Bush explained to my parents, by showing them on a map, how a pattern was evolving over the Auckland metropolitan area of sick babies and children who were all inflicted with the same infection. We were all exhibiting signs of advanced kidney disease. It traversed an area from Mt. Albert to Manurewa, and some went out as far south as Pukekoe, Auckland, and New Zealand. The disease seemed to affect only children under the age of twelve years.

Another female infant from Mt. Albert (her parents owned a poultry farm) and I were the two youngest children affected in New Zealand.

I was nine months old, and the other little girl was just two months older. My body apparently became very swollen, forcing my eyes to nearly completely close. My fingers could scarcely bend, my skin and eyes had turned yellow with jaundice (liver interference), and my kidneys ceased to function so that no urine was being passed, apart from the odd dribble.

My mother confided to me later in my life that she thought she was doing a wonderful job with my potty training, because my nappy was mostly dry, and when I was held out over the potty, I obliged with a small trickle of urine. She felt a sense of pride that I was, in her opinion, nearly potty-trained at only nine months old. She failed to realize that I was retaining urine and swelling up like a blow-fish as the function of my kidneys went spiraling out of control with a gross strep infection.

Following a trip to the doctor, it became a matter of urgency to rush me to hospital immediately. The Auckland Hospital had a ward that was specifically being used for the insurgence of these young patients. On admission, my parents were advised there was a slim chance of my survival, as this condition was life-threatening. Doctor Alice Bush was the resident doctor in charge of this cluster epidemic at that time. (She is now deceased.)

My first abduction was in this hospital—yes, a hospital, of all places. My alien friends must have wanted me to live and do something with this life of mine, because my healing process was miraculous—far beyond the medical capabilities of the day. My health returned without future repercussions or even a hint that anything was ever wrong with my kidneys. Not only that, but my immune system rendered my blood worthy of bottling. My health for the rest of my life has been excellent. To this day, I have never had the need of a family doctor; I don't even have one.

During the time of my first visitation, the nurse had wheeled me in to the treatment room in my cot and left me unattended while she returned to the ward for something—possibly my notes. This was when the three aliens arrived, appearing out of nowhere, materializing through the wall, like something out of *Star Trek*.

A silent, well-organized procedure began to unfold. Two aliens secured me, while the third took the biopsy from my right outer thigh, using an instrument that looked a little like a retracting pen, with claws being revealed and then retracted as the button at the end of the pen was pressed. It was a little thicker than a pen, and it was made of a metallic-looking material. No blood was apparent, and the healing process began immediately, although it left a very large hole in my thigh that I still have today.

My wails brought the nurse hurrying back into the treatment room, where she realized I was being hurt by what appeared to be little children—but instead, they were small, grey, large-headed, wide-eyed, silent creatures, not of this world, dressed in what appeared to be silver suits. The nurse fell against the wall in apparent shock, cowering and dropping to the floor, with her knees against her chin, while her hands covered her face to prevent her from seeing any more. One of the "greys" (as they are commonly called) glided over to her (above the ground) and touched her gently with a probe (I like to call it a wand) on her head. As the wand came into contact with her, she slid from her huddled position in the corner of the room, against the wall, to being completely sprawled out, unconscious on the floor.

It is only now that I realize the power behind this wand they carry and what it is capable of doing. It can stun momentarily, render someone unconscious, administer a complete and permanent amnesiac effect, or cause brain dysfunction and even death. It was a multipurpose tool that could also be used to cut through all manner of substances like wood, steel, and other materials.

The nurse lay unconscious throughout the remainder of the procedure, apparently having been given a permanent amnesia, no doubt protecting her from the memory of what she had inadvertently witnessed. She would have woken to me crying and alone, thereby making her believe she had fainted, with no memory of why.

I too was left with amnesia, but mine was not through the wand, but a normal childhood memory loss to be recalled decades later to enable me to write this book.

Following that visitation, I was left with a huge hole in the side of my leg. I would like to have known how, in my nursing notes, it was explained away by the hospital staff. As a registered nurse now, I can tell you, injections don't leave marks like this. Both Mum and Dad were under the impression that injections were the cause. My parents were not told anything by the hospital staff, but instead assumed it was from the injections I was regularly given to counteract the strep infection in my kidneys. My inquisitiveness was such that forty years later, in the 1990s, I decided to investigate further into my thoughts of abductions, as it was during the 1980s that my interest was piqued.

I approached an x-ray technician in Coffs Harbour, NSW, to examine the deep hole that had been left in my leg. He placed the mobile x-ray unit over the mark, scanning for any hint of bone involvement, but when it was over, he came forth with the conclusion that I had, at some time, years previously, received a punch biopsy. He asked me what it was for, thinking I would know, but I just shrugged my shoulders, pondering the same question of *Why, by whom, and what for?*

I asked if it could have been an abscess or a post-injection infection, but with his experience, he was adamant that a piece of flesh had been removed with no bone involvement. He stated it was a rather sizable punch biopsy and not an infection, leaving a very deep and rounded base. Mind you, he had no idea whatsoever that I had been involved with abductions or aliens. The subject was never raised, so there was no swaying his opinion. What puzzles me now is that I didn't seem to question or worry about any of this all my life. I seemed to accept my parent's explanation of "Your father and I assumed it was caused by injections when you were a baby in the hospital, because you left home with nothing wrong and came home with it, so whatever it was had to have been done in hospital."

I was a New Zealand champion swimmer as a young girl and was constantly being quizzed by both adults and children as to what this hole was on the side of my leg. My answer as a child was simply, "Oh, that's from injections I had as a baby." This answer seemed to satisfy the inquisitive and enquiring minds, and I seemed satisfied with that answer myself, until as a nurse many years later, I realized that injections just don't leave that sort of hole.

It was only in later years I remembered how this mark came to be there, when the scene played out in my mind. I realized that this mark was made during an alien encounter and whilst being a patient in hospital.

Auckland Hospital

YOUR REFERENCE   A 581

IN YOUR REPLY PLEASE QUOTE

Address reply to officer whose
official title appears below signature.
Park Road
Auckland 1. N.Z.
TELEPHONE   FACSIMILE
(09) 797-440   (09) 793 279

12 November 1992

Judy L Clarke

1/11 Nioka Place

Coffs Harbour

N.S.W.

Dear Madam,

In response to your request for copies of hospital records.

The actual records for the year in question, 1952, have been destroyed so are no longer available.

In some cases the hospital has stored some minimal information in the National Archives. I have therefore forwarded your request on to them.

All my life, it was difficult to explain away a mark so obvious, never knowing how it came to be there in the first place.

My investigations went a little further than just the x-ray technician. I also contacted the hospital to obtain access to my hospital records in New Zealand in order to get some type of explanation. These notes, it was hoped, would give me a greater clarity of who found the mark, how they explained where it came from, how it was dressed, if it needed any treatment at all, or if it healed spontaneously straight after the event.

I received a response from the hospital several weeks later, but instead of giving me the information I was after, they instead informed me that my letter had been sent on to the archives department of the Auckland hospital and to expect a response from them in due course. I was excited at the prospect of reading about my care, from my past nursing notes. When I received the letter several weeks later from the Archives Department, they replied very disappointingly, stating that the year in question was unobtainable due to being lost or destroyed. The page they sent me had records available dating back to the early 1930s up to the present day, but it seems the only year that was missing was the year I wanted—1952.

Was this an alien-instigated missing file, deliberately withdrawn from perusal, because all these children may have been young abductees? Or was this purely a run-of-the-mill coincidence? I would love to find out now who those other children were and if they also have biopsy marks on their legs or bodies as well. I still have that archive letter, but have no way of finding out who those other children were.

An addition to the above, entered within hours of writing the previous sentence while editing on 4 December, 2010: I had written an e-mail to a new acquaintance in New Zealand who I was introduced to by Mary Rodwell, who I coincidentally met through her TV program, *My Mother Talks to Aliens* on ABC TV. The lady I was introduced to in New Zealand, is Suzanne Hansen, who happens to be the woman responsible for the release of the New Zealand UFO X-files in December 2010. I told her about the cluster of children in NZ and the possibility of alien intrusion into the disappearance of the hospital files to prevent anyone from investigating this event further. The e-mail response I received today stated (get ready for this), "Oh my God, Judy, I was also one of these children." This made my hair stand on end. We have yet to discuss this. She had to go to an interview and couldn't e-mail more on the subject, so I'm looking forward to delving deeper into this. In fact, I am very tempted to get on a plane and try to investigate in person the list of patients that Dr. Alice Bush was seeing back in the 1950s with this kidney problem.

If more unfolds about this before I finish editing this book, I shall add it to this chapter. Mary is, in fact, flying to New Zealand in February and March of 2011 to take Suzanne deeper with hypnotism to find out more about her abductions. They are also going to try and look into the patient files of Dr. Alice Bush in an effort to find out who these children were and what became of them.

Chapter Three

Manurewa, New Zealand—
Three Years of Age

The next episode of contact, to my recollection, was when I was nearly three years old. We were living in a quaint little house in Coxheads Road, Manurewa, Auckland, New Zealand. It's amazing how good my long-term memory is. You realize that this is a sign of Alzheimer's disease, don't you—when one can remember the past with clarity and not remember things said or done ten minutes ago?

The houses in Coxheads Road occupied one side of the street, because the opposite side was a grassy embankment going up to fenced farmland and vast paddocks—the tall, swaying grass with the wind whistling through it while contented cows grazed. On occasion, my family would often go mushrooming in those paddocks, and our yield gave us delicious mushrooms for many a meal that tasted better than any mushrooms of today.

Our house at the time was flat-roofed, with a monkey puzzle tree taking pride of place in the front yard. The funny thing is that when I visited New Zealand fifty years later, that little house hadn't changed at all, and even the monkey puzzle tree was still there, except it was a lot bigger. The only difference to the property was a subdivision that had taken place some time between us moving and now, reducing the size of the block, while leaving the house completely untouched and in its original state. It was a very surreal experience to see it again. Even though I had only lived there for the first four years of my life, the memories of living there have never left me, including the encounter I experienced one night when I was almost three years old.

This encounter was a nighttime visit, unlike the previous hospital encounter, which was during the day. At this age, I no longer slept in a cot and hadn't for quite some time. My bed was covered with a blue crochet bedspread made by my mother. I can remember during one of my inquisitive moments, I accidentally spilled a bottle of gentian violet on this painstakingly handmade blanket, leaving a big stain in the middle that seeped through to the sheets beneath. I can still see that blue blanket quite clearly. Mum tried everything to get the stain out, but to no avail, so she left it on my bed as a reminder of what gentian violet looked like and what I must never do again. And you know what? I can still remember it from all those years ago. Never underestimate the power of the human mind with its memory; it remembers everything it sees, like a computer—although I cannot remember if I got chastised for the event, but I never forgot the mark.

Upon being put to bed this particular evening, I was somehow transported while still asleep to a craft. I had no trouble going off to sleep as a child. In fact, until my fifties, I could have gone off to sleep on a bed of nails without a problem. Sleep came upon me quickly. There is no recollection of anyone being in the room with me, nor the touch application of the wand to still or quiet me.

As far as I can recall, I slept through the transfer from bed to ship, but I can remember being wakeful and walking around onboard the UFO, with my hand being held. We all know what a two- or three-year-old is like when they are told to stay still. I do remember one particular alien being nurturing and kind to me. It felt feminine in nature and gentle, although there was no definition between male and female (no obvious sexual organs or voice to differentiate one sex from the other). As far as I could tell, they all looked alike, although one could sense the difference through the gentleness and nurturing of the female over the masculine energy. Like us, they all had different characters and personalities. This particular one tilted her head while communicating through my mind, which I now know and recognize as telepathy, but I could feel her compassionate attitude, love, and empathy.

My head was fully extended back, so my eyes could see behind me. Something was being done with my throat, although I had no idea exactly what, but it didn't hurt. I might have experienced pain at the time, but with their methods of amnesia, one forgets if pain had ever been there. I had no recall of pain or discomfort. There was also a loss of time, so I don't know if I they took five minutes or five hours to complete their procedure, even though I was too young to tell the time. There was a void in time. As I began waking with my head still tilted back, there was another human being behind me on a table, having something done to him.

It was a man, because I noticed he had very hairy legs, and one of his pyjama legs was up near his knee. I heard no sounds at all, and he wasn't struggling, so I guess he was asleep. They may have used the wand on him, but I didn't actually see them use it. If I my head wasn't tilted back in that position, I would never have known anyone else was behind me, because it was exceptionally quiet. One of his legs was over-hanging the side of the table—the one with the pyjama leg up—but I didn't see his face, just his striped pyjama pants. I had no further thoughts about his welfare, who he was, or why he was there; I was simply an innocent child, observing without thought, judgment, or question.

I have no recall of the journey back to my bed, simply awaking in the morning, remembering nothing. I was returned safe and sound to my bed (asleep), waking up the following morning as if nothing had ever happened. I am still unaware what was actually done to my throat.

However, I am often brought back to that abduction when I lay on my back and have my neck fully extended—for example, laying back at the hairdresser's, getting my hair washed at the basin, or laying back in the dental chair with the bright light above my head. A glimmer of recall creeps in from time to time, triggered by the little, everyday things that bring back it all back. It doesn't have to be an earth-shattering trigger, just something simple and small. That trip in particular rang bells of star patterns, planets, the night sky, and moving rapidly through the sky.

It was as if I was being given a private tour while receiving an in-depth education, being awake and fully receptive, as a small child, holding on to a gentle alien hand. My question is, why on earth was I shown the universe and taken throughout the craft, only to have it erased? I asked myself, "Was this tour on board the UFO a distraction to keep me quiet and occupied while there were other abductees being examined, or was I being shown around while being given an in-depth education for a reason?"

It seems very strange for even an adult to think that they actually educated and spent quality time with infants and small children on subjects that most adults couldn't understand, but this was a common occurrence, and it was all done telepathically. In other words, what is put in, remains in until needed. Even if my conscious mind had no apparent recall, I know my subconscious mind does, because consciously I have understandings on subjects I have never learned. I have always had a deep attraction to the night sky, and I am innately tuned in to natural disasters, especially earthquakes. I sense when big disasters are about to happen—e.g., the 2004 tsunami, the New Orleans flood in the USA in 2005, and the Australian floods that occurred over Christmas and into the new year in 2011.

Occasionally, I will go through phases of really wanting or needing to paint. I must point out that I am no artist. I will line up the colors that are intuited to me and put the rest away. These are usually white, turquoise blue, and royal blue, and I will be intuited to add some red or yellow on certain paintings. They are basically three-color paintings, but occasionally two more colors may be added spontaneously but with no subject in mind.

My hand paints the pictures while I watch television or listen to music. When I try to bring something into the painting or have something I would like to paint, it is worthy of the rubbish bin; it doesn't work at all. My intuited paintings are all basically of the night sky, planets, UFOs, and the ocean, and some are three-dimensional. One in particular, when it is viewed at different angles, has a face in it that looks like an extraterrestrial, but not everyone can see it. I did not paint this into it; it is simply the brush mark that has been left with no idea of what I was doing—in other words, it was an unintentional, intuited painting.

that looks like an [illegible] material, but in fact everyone can see it. I did not paint this into [illegible] simply the brush mark that has been left with [illegible] what I was doing. In other words, it was an unintentional [illegible]ing.

CHAPTER FOUR

Talking about the 50s—
New Zealand

My parents weren't the slightest bit receptive to the subject of UFOs. The topic wasn't really part of the general consensus; it was a subject not even written about, let alone talked about, because basically, it wasn't real. Even today—but more so back in the 1950s—it's of the belief that "what you can't see isn't there" or "I'll believe it when I see it." I couldn't talk to them, nor did I have the inclination to. In the fifties, this was the norm in most households. Little green men and Martians were the subjects of comic books and nothing more than somebody's wild imagination.

Armstrong hadn't landed on the moon yet, and travel outside of Earth's atmosphere was nothing but a pipe dream at this stage. I think if I would have shared my feelings and views with my folks, my father would have thought me quite insane, ridiculed me, or told me to get my head out of the clouds, which he often did. This subject has never been shared with anyone. The subject of aliens, abductions, or UFOs back in the fifties was not the topic of discussion, and anyone who talked about these things was given a wide birth and was avoided like the plague.

Gentle reminders occurred over the years, and breakthrough memories popped up, but I took it all in my stride. Quite frankly,

I lived with it, never reporting or taking it any further, but all the while knowing I wasn't strange or crazy. I knew what I believed to be truth, but just didn't let it occupy my mind or life. Sometimes what we believe or know to be true is enough. We don't have to discuss it further or involve people who haven't got a clue what we are talking about; there would be no purpose—and in those days, no understanding or belief—plus, what proof could I offer to substantiate my truth?

Even now, I can feel them around when they are in our air space, and those suspicions are usually confirmed by reported sightings in newspapers or are spoken about on television or radio talkback programs. I seem to have some sort of inbuilt sense that alerts me when they are around.

Even though the subject of aliens doesn't scare me at all, it puzzled me through the years, because I had no one or nothing to compare it to. Nevertheless, it felt like I had friends out there, but friends that couldn't be in the same room with me (on earth). Whenever I intuited telepathy, I knew they were in earth's atmosphere.

I am by no means an authority on alien abduction, nor do I claim to know why this happens on a regular basis throughout the world or what their aim is. I can only tell you of my own experiences and my assumptions.

The proof I should have and could have collected along my journey I seem to have treated with ambivalence and complacency, whereby talking about it was a waste of time and would fall on deaf or suspicious ears.

The week I began writing this book, following the approval I sensed I had been given to go ahead, I seemed to not only get back a great deal of the records, diaries, and photos that I had kept and misplaced, but also the words and memories that became so much more fluent. The missing documents, letters, and photos were found in my garage in long-forgotten storage boxes and in the bottoms of drawers. I found this rather timely and quite miraculously coincidental, because I was under the impression everything had been either thrown out or lost.

A statement that comes to mind is "Take the first leap of faith, and the universe will step in to carry you the rest of the way"—and this is exactly what happened. As for the rest of it, this is where your own truth and belief system steps in with an immovable faith or a complete disbelief—but by no means is it insanity, imagination, or a dream. Yes, it's surreal, but it's also very real—in some cases, frighteningly so.

Playing my cards close to my chest all my life by not revealing my experiences about aliens with anyone—not even my parents—I continued to live a normal childhood with little to no changes, although I must admit, one huge benefit I believe to be from my alien friends was my health. With my present nursing background and knowledge, I now recognize that I should never have lived through the diagnosis I had in 1952.

My health miraculously improved from that point to a state of perfection, with no signs of any kidney or liver involvement at all for the rest of my life. I had been rendered asymptomatic (without symptoms), with an immune system that has protected me from all illness for the most part of my life. I have had only five common colds, and all of those were very mild, lasting no longer than three days or so. As a nurse, being in contact with all types of diseases and infections over a forty-year period, I never caught a thing and was never infected with any germs at all. My school and work attendance records were 100 percent, and very rarely have I taken sick time off. I have not been one for "throwing sickies," and most seasonal illnesses didn't seem to get a foot-hold with me. Good health has been my friend throughout my life. This could be just plain good luck, uncanny good health, or a genetic change that prevents disease.

Until my fiftieth year, I had never experienced emotional stress, anxiety, or suffered depression, and for that, I am very grateful. To me, *stress* was a descriptive word; I did not understand fully the true symptomatic feel of it.

However, since turning fifty, beginning with emotional matters of the heart (a broken romance), I too had firsthand experience with depression, plus the effects of work-related anxiety and stress (bullying in the workforce)—and on that, there is nothing worse. I don't feel people fully understand the length of time it takes to recover from bullying, nor the intensity and depth with which it attacks—literally bringing one to his or her knees with the loss of confidence and self-esteem.

My heart goes out to those of you who have had to endure depression and bullying in your everyday lives. I didn't mean to lighten or disregard the effects of depression, it was just that I hadn't experienced it until later in my life, and by golly, it took me a long time to get through it. I chose not to take medications or alcohol; instead, I listened to myself, my thoughts, and my reasons and took note of the lessons. I wrote to myself in a journal about my feelings of anger, disappointment, and sadness. I wrote letters, which were never posted; instead, they were burnt. In effect, this posted the letters to the universe to take charge of. It took some years to return to myself again and become fully empowered, but a great deal of the pain subsided when I began forgiving those who hurt me instead of blaming them.

Amnesia is the main reason why the subject of abduction has had a lid on it for so many years—plus, it cannot be proven, because proof is either taken, forgotten, misplaced, or erased, so when each abductee is returned, they have no memory of what had transpired or knowledge they ever left their beds in the first place. It is a memory most people could not live with and keep their sanity.

For those who scoff at abductees, saying, "Why didn't you grab something—anything—to bring back to prove you were there?" my response to that is, "Abductees are usually paralyzed, so a sleight of hand with anything in reach is out of the question, nor is it possible to take photos from a camera or phone that might have been stuffed into one's pyjama pocket in preparation for the trip. No one knows from year to year or day to day when they are going to be taken. The only things you can move are your eyes, most times. So when each victim is returned, they have no memory of what has happened to them, along with no proof.

In the reported cases of those who have had partial recall, usually they have months or years of nightmares; breakthrough memories; or visits to doctors, psychiatrists, or hypnotherapists to help them reveal what is causing the disturbing sleep patterns and memory flashes. There are very few people who experience an abduction, remember everything that has transpired, and get to wave farewell when they are dropped off at the front door. Rather than explain and risk exposure, everyone is touched with what I like to call a wand or probe, and *voila!* The memory or any subsequent problematic explanations are gone, thereby protecting the victim and, to a larger extent, enabling the cover-up effect of their mission to continue. The entire event is covered by amnesia, and the abduction mission goes right under the carpet with no questions asked.

I would say 100 percent of abductees have no idea where they have been or when they returned, what was done to them, or why. My memories are not all apparent or fluent; they are random and scattered and never fully make sense.

Meanwhile, I have sent telepathic messages out, asking to be left awake and aware when they arrive at my home next time so that can I communicate with them with full memory. I would love this to happen so that some of those burning questions that humankind needs to know can be answered. Regretfully, this has not happened, although I live in hope.

Chapter Five

Papakura, New Zealand—
Four Years of Age

The next visit was two years later, in 1956. I was four years old and living at the Papakura Military Camp in South Auckland with my parents due to my father being a sergeant major in the New Zealand Army. This accommodation was offered to their staff.

My sister (who was nearly three years older than myself) and I slept in the same room on the second storey of a block of two-storied apartments within the military camp. There were four apartments to a block, and we lived on one of the top stories; it was called E block. There were five blocks with grassy areas between the blocks, and each apartment was very spacious and far bigger than most houses, even by today's standards.

Our apartment had three bedrooms, but at this point in time, my sister and I shared the same room. However, some months later, I did end up by moving into the third room to have a room of my own. Stepping forward in time briefly, I feel it important to say that my appearance on a live television show in 1992 regarding alien abduction had me explaining the green room from my abduction to a very talented sketch artist who drew what I am now about to describe for you.

Back in 1956: I went to bed this particular evening, and as I did each night, fell asleep during a slowly declining conversation with my sister. At some time during the night, I was woken to a very bright light in our bedroom from what I believed to be two gentle, silent children taking my hands. We were on a second story, so there is no way a light could possibly shine into our room. It was a pleasant experience and one that didn't frighten me in the slightest. We literally floated across the room and out through the curtain and intact window within a bright beam of light.

I would like to add at this time an assumption regarding my sister and how this occurred with her being in the same room and not being able to recall the event. My sister was a sleepwalker from time to time. Something in her life was obviously causing her some type of deep subconscious reaction—whether it was our strict upbringing, something happening with her at school, or what she, I believe, may have witnessed and traumatically tucked away. I am assuming that she in fact witnessed my return from my sojourn with my little alien friends, which could have filled her with so much fear that she got up and ran to escape what she was witnessing.

This escape took her through the window, behind her bed head, out over the ledge, and hanging from the window sill. Being on the second storey, she climbed out and clung to the sill with her finger tips, with the entire weight of her body hanging down the outside wall of the house with her tippy-toes supporting her weight on a tiny out-jutting on the outer wall.

I believe she was touched with their wand to eradicate the fear of what she had just seen (her baby sister being returned by aliens), and there she was, clinging to save herself from falling with no memory of why she was out there. Our father was returning from an army event, and he glanced up and saw his daughter in her nightie, hanging from the window sill from the second storey. In shock, he yelled out, "Hang on, I'm coming" and did a sprint that would have broken any world record up the stairs and through the house to grab her wrists and pull her inside to safety and his relieved embrace. Naturally, she couldn't remember a thing except a dream she had been woken from, and that was her climbing out her school room window. She was asleep until Dad yelled for her to hang on; it was this that woke her. I, however, was in bed, apparently fast asleep, not stirring at all with the commotion. Was I changed and my void body left in my bed, or was I truly there and simply slept through it all? Was my strange return to my bed what my sister had actually witnessed and was shocked by mid-dream when she bolted out the window? None of us will never truly know. But my sister was so scared by the fact that she had climbed out of the window and could have fallen to her death that she insisted our mother tie her to the bed with stockings, which never happened.

During the abduction, the two little beings took my hands in theirs, and we all rose and very slowly glided across the room and through the closed curtains and window onto what looked like a corridor of bluish-white translucent light. We seemed to glide along the beam into the waiting ship. This light not only formed a walkway or tunnel for us to board, but also surrounded the craft—and in my opinion, this beam made the craft and our entry invisible to onlookers from the ground. This would be the only explanation as to how this sort of thing can happen in the middle of a built-up area without anyone seeing a thing. The craft itself seemed to hover or in fact remain motionless at that height while being completely silent. I know it sounds like something out of *Star Trek,* but at that time, *Star Trek* hadn't even been conceived, nor had *Close Encounters of the Third Kind.*

The appearance of the inside of the craft was familiar with each consequent abduction, making me think I was always taken to the same place each time. Therefore, on arrival, knowing where I was gave me a safe feeling of being somewhere familiar. I felt no fear. In essence, it was similar to having a repeating dream where I knew both the people and the place, but when I awoke, I couldn't remember the dream. I know it was a craft, because the windows revealed endless sky; even though they were facing upward, one could not see directly below. The walls were curved, blending from the floor to a domed ceiling without any corners or joins, and there was hardly an area that was wasted or empty.

I was calm enough to pick up communication between each of them—and not only between them, but also with me on a telepathic level. Nothing was heard at all in speech or background noise; there was an overwhelming silence on board.

Regardless of my age or supposed intelligence, I understood what was going on and everything they were intuiting. They explained (via telepathy) in terms that even as a child, I could comprehend. The workings of the craft, matters of the universe, and anything I was remotely interested in were an education in progress. I realize that sounds bizarre coming from a child so young, but from recall, they treated their abductees who wished to question and learn with respect. However, others who were petrified with fear, screaming, and losing control, for their own safety and that of their captors, were simply put to sleep to alleviate their emotional distress with the required amnesia to prevent ongoing painful memories.

From what I can recall, there were no engines, their power source was from a central column of something that was not gas or air, but more like atmosphere. I cannot explain what the invisible gust of wind I felt in the centre of the craft was, but it was warm and had no smell whatsoever. They intuited to me that it was constantly there and never had to be refueled, was not poisonous or dangerous in any way, and was engineered in a similar way to a circulatory system. It was this that gave them their fuel source—a never-ending supply at no cost.

Their explanations could satisfy a genius, everyday man, child, and infant. Everything they intuited made perfect sense and was easy to understand. It was implanted—understood, if that makes sense. They didn't hesitate to teach if the recipient was open to it, treating the youngest and oldest abductees with intelligence and respect, regardless of age.

We tend to treat our babies and young children in a different way than adults; they do not. They have never been guilty of treating babies and young children in a "cutesy" way as we humans tend to by automatically thinking babies' brains aren't developed enough to understand intelligent data. Perhaps it's because young children look so cute that we use silly baby language and think they can't understand us. Apparently we receive all the information at a young age—more as it is required—and there it remains until it is utilized or needed later in life. Never underestimate the receptive power of an infant or their intelligence.

Going back to my arrival on the ship—the same warm slab and bright overhead lights beamed down upon me. They appeared to be the same aliens, but to tell the truth, they all looked alike—just as penguins, sparrows, and various other species all look alike. I had apparently become resistant and a tad feisty on this occasion, and as a result, a telepathic argument took place between two aliens.

One seemed very impatient and abrupt in nature (I shall call him "he"), and one was a nurturing, kind alien (I shall call her "she"). He argued that I needed the wand to quiet and still me, and she responded by touching me on the forehead gently with her very cool finger (it felt like a frog's skin—cool, damp, and smooth) and saying, "No, she responds well to praise."

Seven little beings surrounded me—three on either side, and one above my head—all reaching the child-like height of around three to four feet tall. They wore what appeared to me to be silver space suits, had no hair, and their noses and lips looked like slits.

They had large, almond-shaped eyes that had no color pigment (just plain black) and no sclera (whites of the eye); therefore, the eye itself did not pivot or move they way our eyes do, nor did they appear to have eyelids. Therefore, they had a steady, almost frightening stare. No hair was seen, no sounds issued from their mouths in speech or breathing, and they possessed only three fingers and a thumb on each hand. Their fingers were slightly bulbous at the fingertips, and I cannot recall seeing fingernails. Due to their inability to speak, their faces were expressionless and lacked emotion, making them appear a little frightening, but they truly are not.

I cannot remember them wearing shoes on their feet, but extensions of their silver suits covered their feet. I had a sense that their feet weren't like ours; they were more like their own hands. I didn't pay too close attention—just a fleeting glance and a sense of it. Because they could pick up every thought, the answers were forthcoming immediately within one's own thinking process. Their limbs were slender and lacking in strength and contour, having no musculature at all, while their heads were large in comparison to their bodies. I attribute this to their ability to utilize far more of their brains than we do, maybe due to the telepathic communication they use.

With the lack of musculature, they had no strength; therefore, any show of strength with a fighting human ended in the use of their wand to quiet the person down. An alien is no match physically for a human.

During this trip, they did something with the crown of my head. No hair was removed, no pain was felt, and no blood was evident. To this day, I am unsure what they were doing—nor do I know what they do to me anytime I am with them—but I saw light flashes and multi-colored sparks, occasional scenes, trillions of symbols, and rapidly moving pictures that I couldn't singularly recognise. Lots and lots of information—similar to a computer download—was happening (education). It was like having an invisible library download.

I was seeing what appeared to be a lightning storm with colors I did not recognize, along with a lot of noise. This noise was not unlike a chain saw or dental drill with a background roar of a jumbo jet all going on in my head at the same time. Whether I was being programmed, I cannot say, but there were adverse effects on my return home, apart from new gifts. The only feeling of discomfort was having to remain in one position for so long. For a young child, it is difficult to keep still at any time. The nurturing female alien gently touched my face with her finger, somehow making me feel calm, safe, and protected, although no words were uttered, just a sense of loving concern.

The alien with masculine energy stood on my right side, concentrating and not appearing to be judgmental or nasty, just steadfast in what his duty required of him.

I believe, as I was told, that the group collective of all seven aliens produced some sort of energy vortex aimed at the recipient to initiate the absorption of necessary information that would be triggered later at certain times in my life (similar to a workable diary). That, accumulatively and to a larger extent, was the reason seven aliens were involved in the procedure. Instrumentation was used, but the driving force was their own energy combined, using their big heads again—telepathy, seven-fold.

The equipment used made way for the implant—but not necessarily a physical implant, if that makes sense. To be honest, even though there were loud noises crashing and banging in my head that were bigger and better than any fireworks display on New Year's Eve, I could not feel where any equipment could have gone into my head, and there were no distinguishing marks that determined the entry point. The entire procedure may have been done on a different level to our physicality.

They explained that not all transplants and insertions into our bodies can be seen; some were mind-triggered (in simple-to-understand language), some were ethereal or telepathically transferred, and their numbers offered the energy needed for this to happen. Some of the physical implants dissolved, others disintegrated and disappeared at certain times, while others had to be removed or replaced.

Once I was returned and time went on, I felt guided reminders that something had been done to me to make me more aware that there were changes or gifts given to me. I often thought, *How did I know that?* or *Where have I heard this before?* or better still, *How come I knew this and no one else did when I've done the same training as others around me?* It worked like intuition. I seemed to intuit earthquakes, disasters, and UFOs. We call it intuition—or is it, in fact, implanted receptors that pick up certain things? This seems to be fading with age. Maybe my implants are corroding.

Their positions surrounding the table also served to prevent me from falling, as there were no rails. He stood in the centre to my right, while she stood near my head to my right. When the overhead light was extinguished, I remember nothing of my movements between their slab and my bed.

I was placed back in my bed, asleep. The return journey had me being transported somehow, but all I know was that I was not walking as I was when we arrived on the craft (floating). All memory of the event just didn't seem to exist until it was meant to much later in my life.

Whatever they did to me each time must have been a carefully planned event, because everything went like clockwork, with no disorder, confusion, or upset at all. Like marching ants, everyone had a purpose, and no one interfered with the other; it was smooth and completely organised. The transporting was done gently, with no force or fight. I would put this down to their telepathic communication. What appeared to be silent was in fact communication through silent telepathy. Even when lying motionless on the warm slab in the craft, unable to move, being fully aware of my surroundings and still able to sense the telepathy and the group conversation, I didn't feel any pain.

I do recall, while still having my head fully extended, a man lying on a slab directly behind me. He was also still and motionless, with one of his pyjama legs up around his knee, exposing his hairy leg, which was hanging over the side of the slab. He was very still and silent, and being unable to see his face, I couldn't recognize him, but gathered that he had been stilled with the wand.

For someone who is full of fear, to suddenly wake up paralyzed in surroundings they do not recognize; being controlled and unable to move while being fully aware; being confronted with alien faces staring relentlessly back with many pairs of large, black, non-blinking, moving, penetrating eyes, in complete silence, while being expressionless, is the stuff nightmares are made of—right? With this fearful situation in mind, the victim of such an event remembers either nothing at all (due to the wand) or snippets of memories that they believe are the result of nightmares, because nothing like this could possibly happen in real life.

As for me, nothing seemed to hurt, but that could have been taken care of with the amnesia at the end of the experience. It is difficult even now to explain what an incoming telepathic message is like. It's not hearing voices—it's not hearing with my ears at all. I believe a deaf person can receive a telepathic message. It is more like a thought—a picturesque, descriptive, all-encompassing thought.

While one is scared out of his or her mind, his or her own mind chatter is going so fast and furious that incoming dialogue is lost in the fear. This is where memories that have returned only return as one's own petrified mind chatter and horror. I forgot to mention that the slab I laid on could be raised, lowered, and also turned over to offer an additional useful work field—like a takeoff seat—when they weren't working on the human condition.

It was apparent by their unfaltering teamwork that they knew at the outset what they had planned to do. They carried out whatever it was quickly, cleanly, and efficiently and then transported me back home to my bed, fast asleep with no memory. I have no idea how long each procedure took or how long I was away from my bed, but my parents and sister never realized I was absent.

Their working area on the ship was not a large working area; it was probably as big as a large bedroom. Every space—floor and walls— was taken up with something; there was no empty space. It had two split levels, as far as I could see.

In addition to the seven little beings that were surrounding me at the slab, there were an additional two sitting at a control console up to my left at a higher level than where I was lying. They were studiously involved with their specific job at hand (it looked like they may have been the pilots) and had no interest whatsoever in looking in my direction at all. The console consisted of a flat area directly in front of them that slanted up and doubled as a desktop or a screen, as things kept flashing onto it.

To the left were shiny, crystalline tubes with pegs that slid into them at varying depths; graphs that came up on a screen; and metallic shapes and symbols etched into different areas. Obviously this was all more interesting than I was, because neither of them once turned to look in my direction.

I could see hieroglyphic signs flashing on the screen, and to the right, beside the flat desktop, was a metallic hand imprint. When sudden movement occurred, it seemed to coincide with their hand being on this imprint. I feel sure they explained all of this to me, because I know too much for it to be just a glance from where I was lying. The two aliens that sat at the console could still see through the windows that ran partway around the craft to the outside view of endless sky and stars.

Upon waking in the morning, I was apparently motionless, staring with open eyes into space, as if in a meditative trance. My father woke me abruptly by slapping me on the cheek and raising his voice, saying, "Stop pretending you are dead; you will scare your mother." He didn't do this to hurt me, but instead to wake me from this scary, trance-like state. It was he who was scared, not my mother, who hadn't even seen me at this stage. It shocked me into a tearful wakefulness because of the sting on my cheek from the slap. It wasn't a hard slap; it was just a shock to be woken in such an abrupt way. I thought I had done something wrong to be woken like this.

Something rather amazing happened from that point onward in my life, but it didn't shock or surprise me, and I didn't tell anyone about it. Upon waking, I could see colors sparking and darting around plants and people (auras). I can still remember telling Mum she was blue, and my sister was surrounded by a brown color with red flecks. All plants gave off a beautiful display of flickering colours. When we are within the aura field of a plant, did you know the plants give us a very special gift, in addition to their beauty and smell? They offer their auras as extensions of their true selves, and this magical, colorful display of invisible light heals both the human condition and themselves. Some people can see auras; they are always there, but just not always visible to the naked eye unless seen through kirlian photography.

When a leaf is torn or broken, it heals itself. Even though the leaf itself cannot be seen as whole and complete, it can clearly be seen by human eyes as complete—but only through kirlian photography. This is the same as an amputee patient when they lose limbs. This is where ghost pains come from. The patient may experience a severe itching or pain where the limb used to be, but in the aura's field, as seen by kirlian photography, the limb remains whole and complete, but invisible to all.

That day also began with another miracle. I woke up remembering my most recent past life, which was the beginning of the return of many of my past life incarnations, as written about in my previous book, *Somewhere in Time*. I can still remember my father leaving the room after he woke me so abruptly. While lying on my bed, turning toward my wardrobe, I stared at the wardrobe door where a wood grain knot seemed to hold my stare. Whether I went off into another trance or meditation, I don't know, but I was "with it" enough to be perfectly aware of what was happening. Maybe my alien friends were giving me my first experience with my past lives that same day to see if their handiwork was how they had planned it. My day one gifts were auras and memories of a past life.

I saw myself as a man—a soldier from the Second World War. I knew my name, and I knew what it felt like to be dressed in heavy battle dress with artillery and a tin cup hanging off me. Even as a five-year-old innocent, I remembered what it felt like to pee standing up. I won't go there at this time, because that life—along with eighteen other past lives—was revealed in my previous book, *Somewhere in Time*.

It was basically how each of my lives was recalled—who I was and what that life was about, who I brought with me into this life, and the lessons I learned from each life, along with what that life means to me now. There is always a reason, a lesson, and an answer staring us in the face; we simply have to recognize it.

This last chapter is a revelation, because even though I had written in my previous book, *Somewhere in Time*, about my father waking me up abruptly with a slap, I didn't quiet piece together that I had in fact just been returned from a UFO sojourn after having flickering lights and loud noises in my head that night before. This was the point in time when everything along a spiritual line began happening. I wrote in the previous book that I knew I awoke with a slap from my father. I knew that was the day when my gifts began, but only now did I add one and one together and realize that the gifts were due to what was done to me the night before on the UFO. It all makes sense now.

The previous night, during the abduction, an adjustment had certainly been made to my psyche, and my attitude to life had evidently opened a spiritual doorway into my past lives. The gifts of healing, vision, understanding, clairvoyance, telepathy, and so much more had been given to me. I had a greater handle on people and could literally feel what they were feeling—and at times, thinking. Due to the fact that I was young, it was not a shock or revelation to me, but a slow and deliberate transition from being an innocent child to being a more aware, gifted, innocent child. Upon waking that morning, I was experiencing something special—a spiritual awakening. To me, it wasn't anything mind-blowing; it was just another experience in life—but not enough to tell my parents or the world. I just let it evolve naturally and quietly.

I came to the conclusion that even a child can achieve anything he or she truly wants to. No matter how big the dream, it can happen. I became aware of the fact that life is fleeting and that I had to cram as much as possible into this life to make up for other lives where I couldn't or didn't get the chance.

Each of us is a creator, just as it has been said by many authors. We have complete control over two things in life—our attitudes and our choices. In addition, our lives here on earth seem so long, so drawn out, and so boring at times, but in reality, they go quickly. Therefore, with this fleeting time, have no regrets. Don't let time rule you. Say you're sorry; forgive those who have hurt you. Live your dreams, love with all your heart, and don't let fear of being hurt creep into your thinking, because after all, time is of the essence.

Life offers us every dream possible in a banquet table of choice. Yet our faith diminishes with guilt, lack of confidence, or a complacent attitude that wastes our time here on earth so we don't fulfill our dreams. Just when we realize the banquet and all the choices we had right in front of us, it's all too late. Each and every one of us possesses a gift—it's called life. Every one of us has drive, enthusiasm, choice, and the ability to heal and love; we just have to believe it. Dare to dream.

I knew intuitively that thoughts and dreams with strong positive desires behind them were the secret of getting what was wanted out of life. It really is no secret; it's an ancient truth. This was all opened unto me as a small child. Such actions as compassion, kindness, forgiveness, understanding, and empathy for others are exactly what we are here for. We are here to love not only the person who stares back at us every day in the mirror, but everyone else on the planet, whether they're black, white, rich, poor, famous, or sick—every one of us has the same opportunities.

My idea of happiness and enthusiasm for my future, I felt, was working with those less fortunate than myself, I wanted to help as many people as I could, especially the underdog—the person who was never validated and the ones who didn't get the chances in life because of their circumstance. This feeling grew with me from childhood to the present day.

I thought I was just an ordinary, everyday kid. Truth be told, I was given a bouquet of gifts that was received as a result of abductions from aliens, with an understanding of what (just for a start) would make our planet survive—e.g., love, peace, caring, forgiveness, etc. It starts with each of us separately. Be courageous enough to care for others, and be courageous enough to forgive those who hurt you. Yes, it does take courage, because others' opinions often get in the way of our own gut instincts. We have to learn to listen to ourselves and not go by others' opinions or judgments. If you could do a good deed a day, could you imagine what this world would be like? And could you imagine how good you would feel about yourself?

The soul within is always perfect, while the body (the covering for the soul) offers an external wrapping for appearance's sake. Our body is in actual fact—an illusive, slowly degenerating clump of cells meant to cover the perfection inside just to get through a lifetime. We are meant to give out to others what we ourselves want, selflessly, lovingly, and happily reaching the other end of life battered and torn, worn out, sagging with wrinkled skin, with parts that have run down or are not working at all, and often times carrying disease before it burns out, ceases to function, and dies.

Like a tree with seasonal leaves that bud, become green and lustrous, and eventually shrivel and fall from their branches to whither, die, and rot on the ground, we are in this cycle of birth and rebirth to evolve into the next seasonal growth. We are cyclical creatures, as all of life is cyclical—including our moon and tidal flows.

The human body simply lives its season (eighty years, plus or minus) of life, but the root system (soul) continues to be there for the next round of life. It is reborn to experience life and everything it has to offer the next time around. Our goal in life is to cram in every moment of living and achievement of our dreams while enjoying every sense we have (sight, hearing, tasting, talking, writing)—to squeeze out every drop of life until the time comes to fall from the tree, whither, and die.

A great extinguished flame who played the lead role in the movie *Ghost* (Patrick Swayze) said in so many words, "When you die, you take all the love you've given and all the love you've received." Apart from knowledge and experience, that is all we can take with us when we pass over. Open your hearts to love coming in and going out so that your baggage on leaving this world is filled with the weight of love. Even in the Bible, another great man said, "Love the Lord your God with all your heart and with all your soul and with all your strength and with all your mind" and "Love your neighbour as yourself" (Luke 10:27, NIV).

This is all you can take with you, so love now, while you can. Don't be scared of the consequences of pain, because they don't really exist. To protect yourself from love for fear of being hurt is to close the doors to life while trying to get through every day without the spark and the enthusiasm that makes you truly happy. When the two become one (the god-self and the mind-self), the body reveals a sense or glow—a feeling of the oneness—that offers perfect, inner, ancient peace. To judge a person by appearance is a sin against that person and oneself—judge not, lest ye be judged. Do the spiritual talk and biblical quotations not demonstrate that alien abductions aren't bad, scary, or evil? They offer insights of the same nature that Jesus Christ himself did. He taught the same wisdom that I have no doubt been given. I was not brought up with any religion, and until I was thirty-three. I had never looked at a Bible—so how was I so aware of biblical meanings and the wisdom of life? This was never humanly taught to me. Yes, I looked through the Bible once when I first acquired one, but I didn't study it.

Getting back to the story—on my return, I owned inner strength, confidence, and knowledge of far more than anyone could possibly understand or realize, but I shared it with no one. I didn't think I was any different from anyone else as a small five-year-old. It's only on looking back that I can see when changes occurred within me. I assumed that everyone felt, knew, and saw what I was now experiencing to be my truth. I might also hasten to say that these gifts were not acquired from imagination. At five years of age, I had absolutely nothing to compare them to, gain the knowledge from, or be told by anyone. I just woke up one morning with an overabundant confidence that I could achieve anything following an alien abduction. I knew more.

CHAPTER SIX

Talk About Telepathy

The aliens I have known don't have the gift of speech—or should I say, the curse of speech? Therefore, they seem not to use any verbal or vocal language, not even noises. Just as humans use varying languages and dialect and force each other to use a different language to communicate effectively when entering a country, aliens also have learned how to communicate with us. Instead of talking out loud, they utilize telepathy, which is a universal silent language, allowing no barriers, mistakes, or misinterpretations with communication.

There are many planets, each having their own dialect. Telepathy is universal, thereby overriding all language barriers, no matter where in the universe anyone comes from. If we all practiced this in our world, there would be no mistakes or misinterpretations. I surmise this is how I can sense when they are around.

From infancy, I was introduced to telepathy, and so with each visitation, this was the way we communicated. For a baby of just under one year of age, having no knowledge of language or words, my thoughts and theirs, were transferred to and from each other, giving me an understanding on a completely different level. Pure thoughts—not thought of as sentences or words, but feelings—were being sent holistically as a sensation and understanding all rolled in to a complete and accurate communication. Instead of using one's ears to hear and intellect to understand what is intuited, a thought is placed directly into one's thinking.

Our languages (worldwide) are dependent upon interpretation, perception, use of words, spelling, comprehension, diction, pronunciation, pitch, language, tone, attitude, and skill, not to mention the hearing-, sight-, and speech-challenged individuals. None of this makes any difference where telepathy is involved.

With telepathy, how the thought is sent is how it is received in total. Human language has many faults, regardless of which continent one comes from. Telepathy is a communication that is 100 percent accurate, unlike any human language. This is a way of communicating that everyone, including parents of young babies, would love to know. One bypasses the learning process, the comprehension, the spelling, and the inability to hear—or, in fact, use any of his or her senses. It would certainly stop the "Chinese whisper" effect that we seem to suffer from, causing all manner of problems and misperceptions with the use of language. If you haven't heard of the Chinese whisper, I will explain just how our human language works.

A line of people are placed in a row, whereupon the first person makes up a sentence and whispers it to the person next to them, and they in turn whisper what they heard to the person standing next to them, until it finally reaches the end of the row. The last person then states what they heard from the person next to them. Nine times out of ten, by the time that message reaches the end of the row, the entire meaning and point is lost in translation and completely different than what the original whisper was. This is how our language can be lost in translation and interpretation. With telepathy, this cannot happen. In effect, languages can do terrible things to the intention of the original message. We have all said something to someone that has been taken the wrong way and misconstrued, causing heartache and confusion. We can ruin the meaning, lose the point, and completely confuse the issue. Then there are tone, emotion, and attitude thrown in on top of that. These offer a personal touch, which skews the entire message, making a pleasant sentence sound angry. A word cocktail and an enhancer of attitude result in whatever someone wants to make of them, while we throw up our arms, saying, "But I did not say that" or "I didn't mean it that way." How frustrating are our words?

With telepathy, one bypasses the learning aspect—it just is what it is. It is wonderful to be completely understood—to have your every thought, word, feeling, and perception received without any mistake or change made at all. Would that not be the perfect communication and teaching tool? No wonder there is so much anger around—our language is sadly lacking in efficiency and effectiveness.

This is the language I knew as a baby. One doesn't have to speak any language in particular to use telepathy. Even a child, baby, or an adult who has never spoken in his or her life can be understood via telepathy. If a recipient has a thinking process, then he or she can communicate. Even now, in some cases, I can understand and can pick up on clear, fearful, worried inner chatter with friends, family, strangers, my patients, and animals. There have been several times when I've been known to ring a friend and the line is engaged because they are ringing me. I have picked up on them wanting to speak to me. No one realizes they are communicating with their thoughts. If practiced, just as human language is, telepathy can be learned.

I suppose it's the same as a child brought up in a household with English, and Italian, for example, is a second language used. That child grows up being fluent in both languages without an accent in either. However, if the Italian language is rarely spoken, the child will speak the commonly used language fluently but will gradually lose all knowledge of the second language as they get older, simply because it is not used on a daily basis. The child will probably get by with an odd word here and there. This is how telepathy sits with me now. I have known it and could use it, but have lost the gist of it because of so little practice.

Telepathy is not linear, visual, or auditory, as our languages are. We string sentence after sentence and word after word, bringing them into play so that only some of the intention of the message is imparted, accepted, heard, comprehended, collated, and remembered.

But we do it every day—hurting people because they got it wrong; being misunderstood because they didn't hear it right; or having the physical inability to pronounce words because of the teeth, tongue, or mental deficits. It's hard work, but we continue to effortlessly do it every single day of our lives, being tripped up with the constant hurts we get from it.

With telepathy, just think of this: we would not need telephones (local, overseas, or for that matter, interplanetary), speech, spelling, schools, education, computers, anything that is associated with the spoken word, thought, or documentation. Language would be silent, just being implanted. There would be no noise, arguments, or anger; therefore, silence would reign, and our world would have far less aggression.

No one could ever tell lies again, so our justice system would no longer be needed. No one could get away with anything. We would indeed be living in a different world if telepathy were utilized in every country of the world. Deafness, blindness, autism, and the inability to speak would not pose a problem to human understanding or communication. Anyone who is able to think can use telepathy.

The concept of this is so out of human thinking that it is difficult to explain, let alone understand. If scientists can't see it or experience it, then it doesn't happen. Many things happen without scientific proof. When mind communicates with mind in the absence of speech, there is 100 percent success in communication. Once the mouth is engaged, we lose credibility. •

Chapter Seven

Communion in the 1980s in Australia

My wake-up call regarding aliens came about during a leisurely day in downtown Sydney, Australia, back in the 1980s. One of my favorite haunts was a major bookstore that had me, as usual, exploring the chances of something exciting I hadn't read. Heading toward my area of interest in the store, I ended up passing a huge promotional book display for a newly released book that stood majestically in the centre of the store. Even from the main door, there was something about this display that seemed familiar to me. As I got closer, I felt a gut-wrenching pull and an overwhelming feeling of *déjà vu,* a step back in time, and one of those internal shocks that jolted right through me. The hundreds of books piled up on the display revealed a face on the cover that sent shivers up my spine and a familiar feeling of "Where have I seen that face before?" Little did I know it was my past stepping up to bite me.

However, as coincidences are part of my everyday life, another one was about to give me a bit of a tap on the shoulder to grab my attention. As I approached the book display, I inadvertently knocked one of the books onto the floor. Hoping like crazy it wouldn't bring the entire book tower down on top of me, I looked around to see if anyone had witnessed my embarrassing *faux pas.* As I bent down to pick the book up, it was apparent there was definitely a connection to my past through this picture. As my eyes met the book cover that was now firmly in my grasp, I took a breath and stopped dead in my tracks. It was a close-up picture or photograph of a huge, bug-eyed, nose-less, lipless face—a face that I knew and recognized. It was the face of an alien. The book was *Communion* by Whitley Streiber.

The hair on the back of my neck stood up, as did the rest of the hair on my entire body. I did a double take while standing dumbfounded in disbelief. My eyes darted around the store, looking for a shop assistant to help me answer the squillions of questions that were dancing around in my head. Finally, I spotted a shop assistant walking in my direction with a box full of books. I waved my arms, with book in hand, to gain her attention. She spotted me. I really don't think she could have missed my flailing arms and blatant facial display of "Help me!" Before long, she was standing before me with her box of books on the floor, asking what she could do to help.

Glancing at the book jacket, pointing, and tapping it questioningly as the familiar face from the cover glared up at me, I frantically and silently questioned myself as to where I had seen this face before. It was an overwhelming feeling of recognition. My first query to the shop assistant was, "Who is this on the book cover?" and "Is it a real person?" Not allowing her time to culminate an answer, I fired a further barrage of uninterrupted questioning at her: "Is this a true story? Who is the author? What country is the author from? What is the book about?" I finally stopped talking, drew breath, and waited in anticipation to hear answers to every question I had just asked her, and more. It was like I had won the jackpot but wasn't present enough to appreciate the prize.

Seeing the face was like recognising someone I knew but couldn't place where from. I needed answers, and I needed them immediately. It was the strangest feeling, and it was very coincidental that I had this book literally fall on to the floor in front of me this way. They say that books jump out at you when you are meant to read them. Wow, now I believe it.

The shop assistant was hesitant to begin answering my questions, probably in case I interrupted her again with additional questioning. She began by briefly telling me it was basically about alien abductions that had been taking place over many years and specifically taking place over the lifetime of the author, Whitley Strieber, who comes from the USA. She went on to say that Whitley Streiber's son was also abducted by the aliens, and there was nothing Streiber could do to prevent it from happening. They would take whoever they wanted, it seemed, and that meant his son. She added that the entire book was written by a very frightened author. She admitted to buying a copy herself, and it scared her to read it because of Streiber's very obvious fear.

The book *Communion* cannot be blamed for my dreaming up experiences, nor for my imagining that I was experiencing the same things as Whitely Streiber claimed to from within his book during his abductions; mine were nothing like his. Streiber's abductions seemed to petrify him with unadulterated fear, whereas mine began from infancy (nine months of age). Maybe this is why I was not so fearful, due to growing up knowing that they were not the enemy.

Needless to say, I made the purchase and couldn't wait to get the book home to read it. Incidentally, the book took no time at all to get through. Everything he had written about seemed so familiar. The aliens weren't scary to me, nor did they invoke nightmares, although as a child, I can still remember the running jumps I used to make onto my bed to avoid being grabbed by some little bogie man hiding beneath the bed, as all children do.

From that point onward, memories started returning to me in snippets, like reminders of my own past. Dreams came fast and furious, and I knew there was a relationship there of sorts between them and myself, but it was puzzling. I knew I had been taken, but I couldn't remember where or when. Tthe face on the book cover had triggered something. It wasn't the contents of the book that triggered me; it was the face on the cover that did it.

CHAPTER EIGHT

Kinesiology and Natural Methods

Moving forward to more recent times—an ex-colleague and good friend, Judy Mune, had been to see a health professional who works at her Currumbin rooms as a kinesiologist, acupuncturist, and alternate health therapist. Following her course of treatments with Heather, Judy offered me one of Heather's business cards and urged me to see her in the hope that she could somehow help me with my fight against fat. This happens to be another one of those wonderful coincidences.

Judy herself had been under Heather's care for various other reasons over a period of time with amazing results. Because of her success, Judy wanted to share this with me and see me gain similar success in my area of need. She had seen my concern over my weight issue that was confronting me. Her recommendation to make an appointment took its time, but eventually, some months later, eventuated.

My first appointment had me filling in a written history form and talking with Heather herself. The master question of why I was there and what my concerns were was going to be her major task. I revealed my weight problem as number one. I had gained one pound per day for thirty-five days while living in Vancouver, and this weight, purely and simply, wanted to take up residence permanently, against my better judgment. I needed answers.

For five years, I had tried diet and exercise, along with a battery of tests and investigations, with all coming up blank. I had the same condition that the *Wheel of Fortune's* Adriana Xenides had been diagnosed with, which was an unnamed disease that eventually caused her demise. They ended up naming it "Adriana's syndrome." The symptoms were abdominal distension, lowered self-esteem, lack of energy, reduced appetite, and her case, pain; however, I—thank goodness—didn't experience pain, but a spiraling increase in weight. I hoped Heather was going to give me the answers I needed.

Muscle testing (kinesiology) is a method of obtaining answers concerning the body and mind directly from the subconsciousness. This is done by pressing an arm, hand, or part of the body that is capable of muscle contraction, which gives the answer by the intensity of the contraction (hence the name "muscle testing"). This test is used to find all kinds of answers to health issues from the mind, body, allergies, and emotions. It's more or less the *why* of what ails the person. I was ignorant as to what was expected in the muscle response; therefore, I couldn't interfere with the answer. In this way, allergies and emotional responses could be sought and found without the person's thinking mind interfering with the way the body reacted.

Once the answers were obtained, she began a series of acupuncture insertions into various areas of my body, none of which were the slightest bit painful. She left me in the room to relax with the needles in place while seeing her next patient. It was during her absence that I went off on a lovely, relaxing meditation while dozing in and out of reality on the table.

The smell of incense and soft music enhanced my relaxation as I drifted in and out of a dream state. Heather returned and adjusted the needles, adding a few additional ones, and left the room again, allowing me to drift back to my wonderful state of deep relaxation. Time disappeared, and before I knew it, I was up and out of there. I experienced a shift—a change, a lightening, and a release of sorts—but nothing that I could claim as a revelation. That was to come.

Judy and I met downstairs following each appointment over a six-week period at a little café two doors down the road and took advantage of our weekly girlie time out for a yummy lunch. Life's too short not to take advantage of these little pleasures. We discussed my progress and her life, as girls do while sitting in the little outdoor restaurant overlooking the ocean. We were lucky enough on one occasion to catch a magnificent pod of whales migrating south, as we enjoyed the food, ambience, company, and the day.

My course of treatments led us to some answers about my weight, but my weight was the reason that brought me to Heather. I didn't have a lot of success and joy in the weight reduction area, but I do believe there was a bigger reason for my visits to Heather. I believe these visits didn't have to do with weight. But I did receive further surprising proof as to my association with aliens regarding the lifetime deal. This continues in the following chapters.

Chapter Nine

Papatoetoe, New Zealand—
Nine Years of Age

It wasn't until the next appointment, when Heather took my treatment to a whole new level, that something quite subtle began to happen. There was a bit of a change in procedure that went like this: following the consent from my subconsciousness my higher self, along with my knowing self, consented to nullify past agreements, contracts, or consent to other beings or selves from this life or previous lives. This was acknowledged by muscle testing; Heather knew that language well. It seems from that moment onward, my memories became clearer, and talking about abductions became something I wanted to do instead of something I was reluctant to do. There was no one who truly understood my abductions and everything they entailed because they hadn't been through it themselves. Conversations were forthcoming, although I feel the recipients tolerated the content with little to no belief, trying desperately to understand because they knew me.

It because exciting and quite cathartic to talk and write about. Unlike the lifelong suppression to express my opinions and experiences, I actually enjoyed letting it out, while the memories became increasingly clearer. It is difficult talking to someone who truly doesn't understand. It's like talking about the color blue when the other person is blind, has never seen the color blue, and cannot remotely understand how to perceive a color they don't know. I have yet to have a conversation about abductions with another abductee. I'm looking forward to that.

Needless to say, Heather checked to see the reason for my forty-kilogram increase in weight gain over a relatively short period of time that didn't seem to want to part company with me. It was revealed that I had indeed been implanted, but apparently it was not a solid implant. She checked the age of the implantation in question. It had apparently occurred at the age of nine in order to offer me various lessons in acceptance, the gaining of knowledge, memory, the enforced reluctance to speak of my experiences, and all manner of things that would serve my greater reason for being here.

Apparently, while this implant was effective, memories and interest concerning abductions were being suppressed, causing ambivalence. The memories were there; they just weren't important enough to discuss. It was like meaningless information that need not be revealed to anyone. Heather's consent to continue went to make all agreements and implant effects dissolved, revoked, cancelled, and negated. We discovered exactly when this implantation had occurred and where in my body. An inner alarm bell rang as I remembered something very strange that had happened to me back in the 1960s. It all seemed to make sense. Suddenly, my memory clarified and demisted, allowing some of the issues in my past that puzzled me then to clarify. I remembered being nine years of age and sunbathing in a pair of blue shorts and midriff top around the side of our garage midmorning one Saturday. The dew was gone, because my towel didn't feel damp when I lay on it. The sun had considerable heat in it for midmorning. Dad was away, working, and I don't know where my sister was, but she wasn't at home. Mum was doing her usual weekend shortbread-baking ritual, along with housecleaning, all of which would keep her occupied and inside the house for the rest of the morning, at least. The area I lay in was sheltered and private, preventing anyone from seeing me, so I felt at ease to roll down my waistband and expose my shoulders. In those days, a tan was the in thing to have and was attractive. Each of us, as kids, would compete for the brownest skin. The idea was to expose as much of my body as possible while keeping as decent as a young lady could.

One minute, I was laying there in my secluded area of the back yard, and the next, I felt the need to get up and get a drink. To my shock and horror, four hours had passed. Had I fallen asleep? With that amount of time in the midday sun, I should have been burned to a crisp, especially with baby oil smothered over me—but I had no sunburn on me whatsoever. There was not even a hint of any differentiation of skin color between the covered and the exposed skin. Instead, when taking my bath later that evening, I noticed two very large white areas about half the size of the palm of my hand over my lower abdomen. They appeared like vitiligo, which is a loss of pigmentation in the skin, making it white. Strange though it may seem, I never showed my mother, and I didn't question it, nor did I discuss it with anyone. I always wondered why, after nine years of age, a birthmark would suddenly appear, especially in the absence of any sunburn whatsoever on any other part of my body when I had been laying in the sun, asleep (so I thought) for four or more hours.

There was no hint of pain or discomfort in the abdominal area at all, but my concern was that after four hours of sunbathing in the midday sun, I would have red sunburn, not white marks. A feeling of disappointment came over me, and maybe even guilt that all this sun exposure might have caused this strange skin discoloration to occur and that I may never be able to show my midriff again. Midriffs were the fashion at that time.

That whitened area on my abdomen remained for over five years. In those days, bikinis came to the waist, so I didn't need to reveal it. By the time bikinis went mini and brief, the marks had gone, much to my relief. The puzzle of those marks always remained with me. Isn't it strange what we accept without question? Now that the alien implant has been removed, I feel I have been given a newfound freedom or permission to write about this subject. It's surprising how many coincidental things have happened since and before that have refreshed themselves in my mind. It feels as if there was some sort of correlation between the negation of the implant, the return of my memory, and the complacency with which I treated the subject. Now I feel an openness to write and talk on the subject with greater clarity.

Chapter Ten

Talking About our Differences

Abductions and UFOs are subjects that have stigma attached. There is avoidance and refusal to engage in this subject. This is due to the ridicule that evolved from those who claimed to have seen UFOs or had been abducted back in the 1940s, before, since, and globally afterward. The assumptions made came across as accusations of craziness, wild imaginations, or down-right lies, and this seemed to stem from the American denial of the UFO crashes that occurred in that country around that time. Their way of dealing with this was by a massive cover-up instigated by the USA government forces. It echoed throughout the world, turning into a global denial that UFOs exist. With this ridicule, it resulted in the general public refusing to come forward to report sightings, thereby achieving the government's goal to stop reports and begin their denial of UFOs, aliens, or life on other planets. The words used to label this are propaganda and denial.

Even now, people are fearful of what they don't understand. Many will not discuss it unless they can show proof, and most times, there is no proof. Those of us who have been abducted may have disjointed memories that play back as a petrifying ordeal, a nightmare, or something strange that lingers in the mind—certainly not a reality. It can't be. It's too different, too unlike what life is all about, too horror movie-ish. With all the indoctrinated whitewash that government bodies tell us, anyone remotely feeling that they may have been abducted has kept it to themselves. Who on earth would reveal this as their truth, knowing what's in store for them?

Have you ever watched a Charlie Chaplin movie where the screen shows a multitude of still shots, making it appear as if it were a moving picture? Take out some of those still shots and continue flicking through the movie, and you will end up with a disjointed and very confusing story that doesn't make much sense. Throw in no dialogue, faces that are hauntingly scary, and only snippets being remembered, and the whole story is thrown into a nightmare and goes to prevent a conclusion where nothing adds up. This leaves the dreamer feeling it wasn't real at all—just a frightening memory that gives hints of fear, because none of it is smooth-flowing or makes sense.

Do these aliens really torture us? My answer to that is not as far as I have experienced. They don't fly to the other side of the universe to torture us and then fly off again. Although a recipient of sampling and testing may see it as torture, their intentions are definitely not to hurt us. Do they take samples from us? Indeed they do. What do they use these samplings for? I am not altogether positive about that, but I do know they have mastered cloning. I also might add to the mix the idea that it may be concerning our genetics—programming, in fact, that protects us. Do they take human semen and eggs? The answer is yes, they do. Do they take skin, muscle, and practically every type of biopsy? Yes, they do. Why? I cannot say for sure. We can all guess and make assumptions, but no one can say for sure. They do happen. It is not to be cruel; in fact, they are more humane than humans. There are many questions I would love to know myself, and if it were possible, I would tell you. I can only make assumptions on the things I don't know for sure. But on the things I can recall, read on.

How do UFOs make it into our air space unnoticed? Because they work on a different dimension—one that our technology or human intelligence has not yet discovered or is unable to recognise. They are radar and physically invisible, although there is satellite footage of UFOs constantly moving around our planet caught on night vision camera.

How do their craft stop in our skies and go backward, forward, up, and down without any sound at all? Once again, their technology is far superior to our own. The metal used in their craft is very light and thin, while being very resilient and nearly indestructible, but stronger than anything we possess. Their power source is based on something likened to a circulation that does not alter with altitude, nor is it affected by gravity. This power source is situated within a central column in the craft and functions silently. It is free of any pollutants, and its source never diminishes.

We use fuel, and on occasion, have to dump it or refuel. Our fuel has a chance of exploding and can be prone to igniting. Well, theirs has none of these limitations or dangers. Theirs is similar to air or atmosphere, but can withstand pressure, freezing temperatures, is not explosive, is not dangerous to breathe, is not polluting, is continuous, never runs out, and costs nothing. Wow, wouldn't we love to get our hands on that?

The controls are manned, usually by two pilots who are experts in using the multifunctional console in front of and above them. I did notice that when their hands came into contact with a hand imprint on the console, the craft turned, tipped to either side, or changed direction. Also situated in the panel were tubes that were sunken in like holes, and into these were pushed crystalline wands at varying depths to initiate functions. On a screen, thousands of symbols displayed, which were instructions or a language I do not know. Most of their means of communication with other pilots both on and beyond the craft were achieved through telepathy.

No microphones, radio, or handsets were used at all; it all seemed very silent. It is very difficult to describe their ship function, because their equipment and means of using it are all so different from anything we have, it's close to being incomprehensible. We have nothing to compare it to. As an air hostess in the early 1970s, I have seen the flight deck of our aircraft, and there are no similarities or comparisons whatsoever. I can only describe what I witnessed on their craft. They go beyond scientific proof, because what cannot be tested can reveal no results. Just because we cannot hear or see them does not mean they are non-existent.

Our scientists work on a specific level, while our alien friends work on a completely different level or plane. They aren't magical creatures, just technologically more advanced than we can understand. They are in our skies, but we cannot see them. Just because a blind man cannot see does not mean there is nothing to see.

In the same way, our scientists appear to think along the same line (seeing is believing), and this tends to put the brakes on advancement, because they refuse to believe anyone else occupies our air space but us until it can be proven. We lack the skills and technology to find them, but that doesn't mean they aren't there. This, in my opinion, is blind ignorance and very presumptuous. Do we really think that our state-of-the-art equipment is the only equipment that can be used to track them? I think not.

They don't look, speak, move, or dress the way we do, nor do they communicate, reproduce, eat, or travel the way we do. Therefore, with the differences between them and us, it seems to make them non-existent, in our opinion. It is an obvious observation that we don't accept differences easily, nor do we accept anything without scientific proof. Although God and Jesus Christ are two entities no one on earth has ever been in contact with, we have blind faith that both exist or have existed. UFOs have been written about, just as the Bible has, and yet one is blindly believed; the other is rejected. The one that is rejected has been witnessed. There are sightings every week of UFOs, yet Jesus and God have not been witnessed at all; they are only hearsay.

Governments in many countries do have proof of alien existence. We have footage of their craft. But still, they dictate to the world that aliens and unidentified flying objects do not exist. If they did land, would our governments shake their hands, say their pleasantries, and bid them farewell? I don't think so.

They would be arrested, interrogated, and imprisoned in a locked unit or military base with a barrage of tests and samplings carried out on them. Even though they test us, we are treated with respect and returned with amnesia so as not to remember what is done to us or any discomfort we may have experienced. This is mainly for our own protection—and, of course, theirs. Would we return them, let them go free, and watch them fly into the skies on their homeward journey? The answer to that is a resounding *no*. We would not allow them to return to their home planet, but would continue testing and observing them until the end of their lives. They would be drained of any knowledge, and then we would autopsy them when we were done with them. Does that make them or us more humane?

We, the human race, are far more threatening and dangerous to our planet and universe than anyone else; therefore, we are deliberately being left in the dark for our own safety, longevity, and protection. This is why they will not approach us or reveal themselves. Maybe when we change, they will arrive.

Our genetic makeup is changing. We are becoming a taller species, and because of our diet, we are unhealthier than previous generations. Our earth is becoming contaminated, as are our skies and oceans. We eat more fats and sugars, and our food is overprocessed, preserved, and genetically changed, mainly because of our desire for wealth. The longer the food lasts, the more money is made, and this comes at the cost of our health and lives. With all the changes that are happening on our planet and in our universe, we are being observed. The sad thing is, we are destroying our planet singlehandedly, and we *can* stop this, but greed for money and possessions is getting in the way.

There is much written and hidden on the subject of governmental meetings, alien captives, agreements, photographs, and samples taken from both craft and creatures. These X-files are beginning to be released now in various countries, proving that UFOs do exist and our governments know this. There are civilizations other than our own out there in deep space. With the proof America has on the Roswell incident and others, we *do* have positive proof that UFOs exist. To fly these craft, there have to be pilots. These pilots, who are not citizens of earth, are called aliens; therefore, aliens do exist. Due to the fact that I have insufficient proof of this myself, I shall move on from what might or might not be fact or fiction. I will, however, discuss instead my own interpretation of things, my own story, and how that has unfolded over my lifetime.

We seem to be filled with fear and anger about subjects we don't fully understand. With the adverse publicity that had been circulated during pre- and post-war times along the UFO line, the subject was hidden whitewashed, and ignored, as far as the public was concerned. However, what went on behind the closed doors of military installations is whole different story. Thank God for whistleblowers.

It's about time that at least one singular experience is revealed to show the world that they are not as scary or as bad as people first thought.

We are not managing our own planet very well at all, so maybe we are being prevented from trying to get a foothold on other planets, because we are a very irresponsible species. For example, we carry atomic weapons on board our space craft when our rockets go into deep space, and when we land upon other planets, we tend to take ownership by planting a flagpole in the ground, claiming it as ours. Hullo? We don't even own the planet we live on; we occupy it. Earth has been given to us to take care of, not own. But sadly, the greed is taking over, and we are bleeding our Mother Earth dry of all her valuable commodities and resources—draining and drilling.

Allow me to describe a similarly: When a perfectly balanced sphere that sits in its position in the cosmos tilts, why would that happen? Could it be that the perfection and the integrity of the sphere is cored out by man's greed, and this is causing earthquakes to resettle her and shift her balance to maintain her equilibrium? Could this be due to changes in her tidal flows, weather patterns, olobal warming, perhaps? Mining may be beneficial to some, but it may end up being detrimental to the multitudes. A sphere cannot remain a sphere if its core is drained.

These aliens, I believe, are distantly related to us. At some time in our evolution, an agreement was made to allow what now goes on between us, but through birth and time, we have forgotten that contract. It is all part of our destiny as a race, a planet, and a progressing life form; it has nothing to do with personal relationships. Evolution and our planet's protection and place within the cosmos are part of life. They have been going on for eons, and there is nothing new about it. Yes, it seems invasive, Yes, it can cause all manner of issues with acceptance, truth, fear, and realism on a personal level—but when push comes to shove, it is happening and will be for a long time to come.

CHAPTER ELEVEN

Talk About Kinesiology Treatment

When I was nine years old at my home in Papatoetoe, Auckland, New Zealand, I was sunbathing outside near the garage. I later discovered two white patches on my lower abdomen. The reason for those two white marks is a mystery to me, but if I were to take note, maybe the reason for my trip to Heather, the alternate health specialist, tied in with more than just my weight problem. Was this the reason for meeting Heather? Was my weight the reason for the nine-year-old implantation? Was the implant working on a time release? Was it the reason that took me to her to have the implant of forgetfulness and complacency cancelled, enabling the truth to be told in a book? Could it be that easy or that far-fetched?

The reason for the white patches could be anything as far-fetched as taking my young eggs for harvesting or for cloning; this will never be truly known. As I said earlier, I don't pretend to be an authority or have all the answers to everything they do. I wish I did, but they surely wouldn't do this without any reason at all or just for the fun of it. The fact that I was left with those white marks tells me without a doubt that something was done to me within that four-hour period in the midday sun—in the words of Budd Hopkins, missing time.

Who really knows what went on inside me—or for that matter, the reasons why? I can, however, recall with amazement going to bed that night and pulling the sheets up over my head. When I went to roll over, as my body turned, my arm rubbed against the upper sheet, causing the entire top sheet to light up. I then realized that whenever I rubbed the sheet with my outstretched arm or leg, this caused friction on the sheet, resulting in an illumination so bright I could have read a book by its light. I tried this over the following weeks each night. This action produced a lesser and lesser effect, proving to me that at the time those white marks were left, I was left with some sort of energy I didn't usually have, possibly causing an electromagnetic current to remain in my body. The point to note with this is that they both occurred at the same time, one being an effect (the white marks) and one being an aftereffect (the magnetic energy I was left with).

Thinking out loud about additional reasons for the white patches, I was never a sufferer of PMT or pain. Throughout my entire fertile lifespan, I never experienced cramping or period problems at all. I had no problems conceiving my son; he was a planned event, down to the very night my husband and I planned to conceive. Being a newly trained midwife at the time, just returning back from my training in Scotland, I knew my body and my cycle well. Therefore, planning our pregnancy and being successful in the outcome was a blessing to have been achieved so easily. Both my new husband and I were thirty years old and decided that seeing as we had been married for six months, we might as well start trying to have a baby, just in case we couldn't. We achieved our goal on our first try. My health was perfect, as was my immune system. Basically, I was the epitome of health as a girl, as a young woman, and for that matter, as an old lady.

However, in my fifties, my abdomen became very distended, which seemed to coincide with a period of emotional heartbreak and stress in the extreme. In addition, there was a weakened area in my musculature in my central abdomen (rectus abdomenus) that resulted in three herniations forming. These were eventually operated on in December of 2010. Heather agreed that nothing happens for nothing, and the outcome we most expect is quite often not the outcome that actually happens and counts for something. My trip to her could very well have been the steps that brought me to now. I truly believe it was to disarm an etheric implant so the curtain of vagueness was dropped, so to speak, to enable this book to be written. Who knows? Maybe the hernia operation had a part to play in this as well.

In early December of 2010, it became rather urgent that I was admitted to hospital to have a repair of a large hernation. Several central abdominal herniations were found at the time. This had me lying on the operating table for two hours. The three-inch midline subcuticular suture line went from my umbilicus upward. The miracle of miracles was that this was major surgery, and I felt no pain or the slightest discomfort at all. The healing occurred within one week. I was actually discharged home seventeen hours following the operation and had no medications apart from twenty-four hours of self-administered paracetemol just in case I experienced pain. The pain never came, so I ceased to take anything after twenty-four hours. My surgeon said I required no follow-up apart from a visit to my family doctor if I needed to. (I don't even have a family doctor, due to my good health.) I never did have a follow-up for it, and it was as if I had never been operated on.

My healing process was absolutely miraculous—beyond normal— with an exceptional pain threshold. Even the anaesthetist said to me pre-operatively, "Judy, this is no small operation. You will feel pain for quite some time afterward, so please tell me what you would like for pain relief for your post-operative period." Being a registered nurse, I knew the options, all of which I refused. The very next morning, I got up at 5:00 a.m., had a shower, got dressed, put makeup on, ate a small breakfast, and waited for my surgeon to do her rounds. As I waited, I walked up and down the long hospital corridors, feeling absolutely wonderful with no twinges, aches, or pain at all. She took one look at me and said, "You look so good, I thought you were a visitor." After a brief check that the outcome of the operation was what she expected, she consented to my release. She then added, "You can go home now if you like. Have you got someone to pick you up?" I lied and said yes. Feeling no pain at all and going against the rules (being the stubborn girl I am), I put on my backpack and walked out of the ward to the car park and drove myself home. I had parked my car overnight in the hospital grounds.

Having no drugs in my system and feeling no pain at all, I drove myself to a relaxing recuperative period in the comfort of my own home. It was an amazing experience to be so pain-free with no drug assistance at all. It was my first major operation, and I hope my only one.

Could my genetics have been changed, adjusted, or fortified as the baby who was tampered with in the hospital in the 1950s? It was just not normal to have such a large operation and have such miraculous healing powers with no pain—plus my entire life of good health. I must say, I am not complaining; it's just puzzling, but pleasantly so.

I've tried every diet known to man: juice fasting, protein diets, CHO diets, a balanced diet, and smaller meals, along with diet fads in between. I bought a one-year membership to a women's gym, as everyone kept telling me that exercise and energy must exceed food intake. I went on a strict, seven-month gym exercise regime, going six days a week for one to two hours every day, sweating my guts out, doing weights twice a week and cardio every day. I had consultations with various dieticians (three in total), and guess how much weight I lost in seven months? None. Guess how many centimeters I lost? None. My intake was minimal while eating very nutritious food, but my appetite had diminished to the extent of not feeling hungry. When I did eat, I filled up quickly. I had heartburn following anything I ate and drank, including water. Many friends, neighbours, professionals, and family members have jumped on the bandwagon, saying, "You can't stop eating regular meals. You have to have breakfast, lunch, and dinner—if not, even six small meals a day to lift your metabolism, otherwise your body will go into starvation mode, and your metabolism will drop, and your body will hold on to all the weight." Well! "ppphhhffftt" in answer to that.

Auschwitz prisoners went into the prison camps and were fed one to two very small meals a day. Over a one- to four-year period, none of them came out hanging on to their fat in starvation mode.If they were lucky enough to even survive, they came out looking like living skeletons. I have been eating this minimal amount and have supposedly been in starvation mode for six years. Surely something would have dropped off—but alas, no.

In addition, if I were to have a lap band (which is for people who overeat), that would throw me into starvation mode by minimizing my quantity of intake down to even less than I eat now. If one maintains a starvation mode (as in the prisoners of war), one must lose weight, as shown in our history books. I rest my case.

A very nasty and unprofessional local doctor once said to me, when I asked for help along the weight line, "Every fat woman says it's not what she is eating." Needless to say, I very rapidly lost respect for him, and I still don't have a family doctor.

You may very well ask, "What would aliens do this to you for? Why would this affect you fifty years later?" My answer to that would be that on the one hand, those white patches may have nothing at all to do with my bowel function or present weight problem, fertility, or anything at all, for that matter. On the other hand, they could very well have everything to do with it. They could have caused a time-released slowing down of peristalsis to offer a lesson in acceptance, humility, and loving myself fully and completely, regardless of how I appear to myself or others.

Each of us can be dealt bad hands in life, but this is not for punishment; it's merely to give us the opportunity to change our own attitudes. We have an opportunity to take a different path or just accept our lot in life. The weight itself may have been the means to visit Heather, but not necessarily to fix it. Instead, maybe I was to be given the key to an awakening by invoking the memories of my past abductions and releasing past contracts so I could write this book. Does this sound far-fetched? It could very well be, but it is also in the realm of possibility.

Getting off the subject of bowels and back onto the track of abductions, I somehow have God-given gifts along the lines of psychic intuition, automatic writing (the same type of thing as conversations with God, using nearly the same words), healing, the ability to be able to jump into someone's psyche to pick up how they are feeling (medical intuition), psychometry, and clairaudience. I have a keen intuition, but very seldom do I use these gifts, except when I am guided to do so.

When I do use the spiritual gifts I've been given, it is not for money, praise, proof, or ego. In fact, I don't choose who I heal or who I talk to with channelled information. I don't tell anyone what I do. It is done silently, spontaneously, and with guided reason, and on that I do not question it.

Being a beauty therapist, I cannot count how many of my clients, following a facial, react by stating out loud, "What did you do that caused such beautiful colors? I've never seen such vibrant colors before." We are given gifts, and these go out to whomever for whatever reason. I do know all my clients leave my clinic very much calmed (but not necessarily cured), contented, and pleased with their skin and faces.

Whether there was a lapse in actual abductions or whether there was a lapse in my own memory of them, strange occurrences or coincidences started to occur that were very much along religious and spiritual lines. One only has to take notice of life's chain of events to see the miracles behind them. It's actually been noted that most alien abductees have gifts, and these gifts are usually those of healing, artistic talents, painting, poetry, writing, expressions in carving, sculpture, and anything creative and artistic. They are also more into natural therapy and caring, nurturing jobs. Are you recognizing yourself yet?

Chapter Twelve

Howick, NZ, 1972—My Pledge to Serve

Following a broken engagement in 1972, I returned to New Zealand for an extended working holiday, staying with my parents. Some more weird and wonderful things began to occur that made me wonder, *Was this a deliberate ploy to have me return to where it all started for a continuation of my growth along the spiritual line? Did the spiritual aspects indeed have a link-in with our ET friends?* The telepathic messages I seemed to receive had an outcome that was definitely guiding me toward a spiritual path. It was like a God-link.

I was driving out to a friend's place in farmland on the way toward Howick, with a backdrop of rolling hills, and in the forefront was fenced flatland with tall grass swaying in the wind. Passing a quaint little church up on the hill to my left, I found the exit side road leading to my destination. Further up the road on my right, I pulled over to the side of the road at the base of the foothills. It was quite a surreal feeling, with not a soul in sight. Opening the car door open, I stood in the middle of the road while the door remained open.

Even though I was not brought up under any religious affiliation, I had an inbuilt knowledge of and respect for God or a presence that was able to hear my every thought. I don't know where this came from, because my family didn't discuss any religious topics in our house at all. It may have had something to do with the friend I was about to visit. He was associated with a spiritualist church as both a healer and speaker, so I might have had spiritual thoughts in mind as I approached his place. Nevertheless, my thoughts, the visual layout of the land in front of me, the eerie wind whistling through the fields, and the dull outlook all made me want to step outside the boundaries of my car and drink in that feeling and the sight of my surrounds. I parked my car on the grassy embankment beside the road and stood motionless with my eyes closed, feeling the wind on my face. I felt close to this presence, whatever it was.

There was a peaceful feeling. I heard the wind whistling over the long grass, which swayed in unison for as far as the eye could see. Each blade of grass joined as one, like a magnificent, unified, moving ocean in a magnificent dance. My car door was open. As I stood with arms outstretched in the middle of the road, not a car, a cow, or a soul was in sight. There was just an eerie silence with the whistle of the wind. I looked up toward the sky and began slowly spinning around with my palms facing upward, reciting a promise as if someone or something up there had been waiting to hear it all my life. With my eyes closed, I said out loud, "God, I give myself to you, now and forever. Please guide me through my life to do your will and not mine, to serve humanity. I am yours in service for the good of all, for the rest of my life. Amen." The grass became still, an erie silence issued all around me, and I felt recognition of my dedication to serve. Returning to my car, I started the engine and continued on my journey up the hill to meet with my friend. Later in the evening, I returned home again.

The very next day, I went to Pakuranga, where I worked in a pharmacy in the shopping centre as a Karitane Mothercraft nurse, helping young mothers with their babies while also serving in the shop. That day, just before lunch, an elderly lady hobbled in, appearing very frail and very shaky (she had Parkinson's disease). She tried to find something in her handbag. She spent quite some time searching for whatever it was she was looking for when I approached her, offering to help. She was looking for her shopping list. In nearly illegible writing on her paper was a long list of groceries and just two items required from the pharmacy.

Dragging a chair from the back of the shop, I sat her down and got the two items that were on her list, wrapping them and popping them in a bag along with the receipt. Seeing her fragile demeanor and the length of her shopping list, I couldn't let her go out of the shop without offering to go to the supermarket for her to do her grocery shopping (in the middle of my working day). She accepted gracefully while remaining in the pharmacy on the chair. I darted through the aisles of the supermarket next door, filling her shopping needs.

Upon my return to the store, I walked her to the taxi stand and helped her into an available cab, along with her bags of groceries, and sent her on her way. Thinking nothing more of it, I returned to the shop and continued my work. My boss was a kindly man, Murray Dunn. I had known him for quite some time, as I had worked as a Karitane Mothercraft nurse privately, caring for his own lovely three children in their home just the year before (like a nanny).

He called me to his office and asked me to sit, saying he had to talk to me about an observation he had made earlier that day. He admitted to observing me with the elderly customer I had earlier that morning. He went on to tell me I was wasting my time working for him in the pharmacy and that I was better suited to a nursing job. I burst into tears at the thought of being sacked from a job by a man I had a great deal of respect for.

So I asked him, "Why are you sacking me?"

He replied, with a smile on his face, "Goodness me, no, I'm not sacking you. I will even find you a position myself that is better suited to you. This job does not do you justice. You are a born nurse, Judy." He continued, "No, Judy, I am not sacking you. You need to work with people who need you as a nurse."

"But I want to work here," I pleaded.

"Leave it to me. I'll find you a job that is better for you than being a shop assistance," he said.

Later that week, he gave me the phone number of a place I had never heard of in Epsom before. The place was called The Reception Centre.

It was a big converted house in Epsom, Auckland, in an ordinary street that functioned as a safety halfway house for beaten, abused, and abandoned children, some of whom could not be adopted out to loving homes because of the defects they had either sustained through birth or incident or because there was an inability to find the parents to acquire the necessary signatures to relinquish the child for adoption. Instead, these poor, unwanted, unloved children became wards of the state.

In effect, these parents displayed by example, "I don't want you, but I don't want anyone else to have you, either." It was all very sad. I followed Murray's instruction and made an appointment to see the Matron of the Reception Centre to apply for a position there as a Karitane Mothercraft nurse. I was successful in my application for the position and left the employ of Murray Dunn at his pharmacy. I was the only trained member of staff there; everyone else was either a cleaner, cook, carer, or nurse's aid. There is a reason I say this, as you will find out shortly.

There was one little boy in particular who caught my eye. He was just adorable, with blonde hair and sparkling blue eyes. Due to a hole in his heart, he could not be adopted out. He was signed over as a ward of the state, but due to his cardiac anomaly, which I thought was grossly unfair, he was denied a permanent home. His mother was serving time in jail for abusing him, and the person who was fostering him had been guilty of neglecting him. So at the tender age of two, this poor little boy had experienced a dreadful start to his life and was now institutionalized, waiting to be tossed from family to family for the rest of his young, fragile life as a foster child until he reached the age where he could make his own way in the world.

Each day, as the tiny tots were put down for their naps following lunch, the older children were asked to play quietly. I decided it was time to step in. It was during these nap times that I was guided to stand beside his cot while he slept. I'd hold my hands over his chest in an effort to transfer healing from the universal source or God through me to heal his little heart so that he could be returned to good health and adopted into a loving family for a normal, healthy life, giving him a chance. Each day at the same time, my hands did the work they were guided to do. I cannot in all honesty take any credit for this healing, because I was simply a vessel for the healing to pass through to this lovely little boy.

His little face winced, and his body twisted in obvious discomfort as my hands began to heat up while not even touching him. Thankfully, he never woke up during the healing. After two weeks of daily bedside appointments, which no one knew anything about, he was sent for his regular scans to check on his condition, which he was due for at this stage.

I happened to be in the Matron's office on the day the little boy's results were about to be discussed between herself and the child's doctor. I was searching in the office cupboard for a key when they began their discussion. The doctor was openly amazed and very excited to find that the scans revealed a completely healed heart (with no scar tissue at all). He found this quite unbelievable, when for all of this boy's two years of life, his condition had shown no signs of improvement or change. Now he was completely and perfectly healed.

The resultant action was such that this little fellow was able to be adopted and to live a normal and hopefully happier life in the future. The doctor, with a smile on his face, hit the table with his hand and looked at the matron, saying, "Put in his application for adoption." This is how God works, in very mysterious ways. I had given myself in service just several days before, and already I was being guided to serve. I was happy.

In short, this chain reaction went something like this: I offered myself in service to God by going to work and helping an old lady with her shopping. I was seen by the boss. I was moved to a new job (to serve God). This enabled a child to be healed. He was put in a home where he could be loved like any other normal child should. Can you not see the chain reaction here?

Shortly after this child was recognized as being adoptable, I was forced to leave this job due to being placed in the kitchen as a cook. While being the only trained member of staff there, I was taken from the wards and the care of the children to be a cook, so I resigned in disgust. This is when the required job by God was successfully completed. When you offer yourself in service, you are placed in a position to serve, and sometimes those places are not altogether pleasant. That is when I returned to Australia. As you can see, I was only meant to be there to initiate the healing of the child and then move on.

CHAPTER THIRTEEN

Bibles and the Power of Prayer—1985

I awoke one morning in 1985, having written on a piece of paper a dream I had earlier that night. It had always been a habit that I keep a pencil and paper on my bedside table in case of thoughts or dreams that I may have during the night.

I had woken with the words *Corinthians* written on my piece of paper, and I had no idea what it meant. It is a known fact that in the morning, once we wake and move, our dreams disappear. I use a pencil instead of a pen, because a pen might block, depending on the angle at which one writes (in the dark, with eyes half-closed) whereas a pencil writes continuously, regardless of angle—plus, no ink will run onto the bed.

Waking to find *Corinthians* written on my paper was a bit of a puzzle. The only thoughts that ran through my non-religious mind as to what that could mean was Corinthian doors. I rang my girlfriend, Geraldine, and during the course of our conversation, I mentioned that I had woken in the night to write down the word *Corinthians*. I asked her if she knew of any other meaning than Corinthian doors. She laughed and said, "Judy, that is one of the chapters in the Bible." Geraldine had practiced earlier in her life as a Catholic, whereas I was brought up without a structured religion. My father was from the Church of England, and my mother was Jewish. My sister and

I were bought up without religion at all, giving us the freedom to choose our own as we matured. At no time in my life had I ever read or seen the Bible. Geraldine explained that both Corinthians 1 and 11 were in the Bible.

"Oh," I said, "I've never read the Bible. In fact, I don't even own a Bible; do you?"

"Yes, you can borrow mine, if I can find it," she laughed.

I knew that I was supposed to be getting a message that I clearly did not understand, so I said out loud, after I had hung up from our telephone conversation, "God, I need a Bible of my own. Where do I find one?" Even though I was not religious, I had a strong faith of an all-hearing, all-knowing God that I could call on anytime I needed him, as if I had a hotline to God. Where did that come from?

Within two hours of that little request, there was knock at my door. Geraldine had dropped in on her way, leaving her Bible for me to look at (Bible number one). Then, shortly after she left, there came another knock at my door. It was a smartly dressed young man, holding a beautiful black, leather-bound, gold-leafed Bible. He said good morning and continued with his obviously rehearsed dialogue that went something like, "I have a beautiful Bible here that can be yours for free. All you have to do is sign up for three Bible classes, and it's all yours" (Bible number two). I glanced through it and noticed that even though it was beautiful, I could hardly understand a word of it. I told the man that it was strange wording, even though it was in English. He revealed to me that it was a King James Version, admitting it was a hard-to-understand version of the English language. I could hardly believe that my prayer only a few hours ago could have been heard and answered within such a short space of time. I agreed to the course only because I could see a direct response from God, and it was my job to accept it without conditions or question.

That's not all. The rest of that day turned into miracle after miracle, and by day's end, I was in receipt of four Bibles. After agreeing to have the three lessons (just to get the Bible), I took my young son shopping. Before we left the house, I decided to check the mailbox, and in the box was a beautiful postcard with a picture of Jesus Christ with his arms outstretched, surrounded by animals and young children. Written on the back of it was an obligation-free offer for yet another Bible (Bible number three). When Matthew, my son, and I reached the shops, we were walking past a Mall at Dee Why square, and I paused momentarily on the footpath to check my shopping list. During my search for my shopping list, I had inadvertently stopped outside a shop I had never really noticed before—a religious shop.

A woman who was obviously working in this shop walked up to me on the foot path and took my hand. (This is something not heard of today; that's for sure.) I struggled with the stroller with one hand and followed her into the shop. She said something that blew my socks off: "I have something for you. This one is so much easier for you to understand than the King Charles version. Come inside; please follow me." I pulled Matthew's stroller in behind me and followed her into the shop, where she disappeared out the back for a few minutes. We waited at the counter for her to reappear again, and when she returned, she was holding a pink book in hand, saying, "The King Charles version is too hard to understand. I felt this one was for you. Please take it; there is no charge" (Bible number four). She spoke to me from the moment I met her on the sidewalk as if she knew what had happened that morning. I was completely blown away.

My first thought was, "Am I being listened to with my every thought? How did she know I couldn't understand the King James Version I had just received?" Needless to say, I did read it from cover to cover and found it far easier to understand than the King Charles version—at least, understanding it to my own ability, making my own interpretation. I found Corinthians 1 and 11, and even though it covered a subject I was going through at the time, I felt this whole event was simply a testimony to God's power to deliver an answer to a prayer and perhaps make me realize that I am being validated by what I pray for.

I am quite fascinated by the fact that depending upon each person's level of understanding, we all interpret the Bible at different levels. Each religious church body puts a different meaning or slant on any given part of the Bible, so depending upon what denomination you are, there will be a different interpretation on the same words—hence, the reason for Bible studies. This brings everything to the same meaning. I choose to make up my own mind and work at my own level of understanding. My interpretation is the only one that I will accept. In saying that, I am open to hearing other people's points of view.

Chapter Fourteen

August, 1987—Harmonic Convergence

My recollection of the Harmonic Convergence on 16 August, 1987 is still quite vivid in my mind as the beginning of a keen interest along the spiritual line—like a page being turned from one chapter in my life very clearly to the next.

I was preoccupied in the back room of my home, doing some menial task, when my four-year-old son, Matthew, came running to me excitedly, revealing something most children wouldn't be able to understand, let alone convey in such an intelligent manner. He had evidently heard a news broadcast on TV about a worldwide gathering of people in various countries celebrating the Harmonic Convergence, and Bronte Beach was going to be Sydney's gathering place for this spiritual celebration.

This was all about the alignment of the planets and was last seen quite some years ago. It was supposed to bring a shift in humanity's spiritual awakening. I couldn't believe my four-year-old son would even think to take notice of an event so completely out of a child's understanding. This alone made me wonder if perhaps this was a sign that I was meant to be there. I waited for the next newscast for more information. When it came on, I took note of the phone number that was given out. I dialed the number, fully expecting the line to be busy for hours. A man answered and explained what the Convergence was all about and that it was being celebrated in various areas all over the world. Sydney's place of choice was to be on Bronte Beach. Anyone who wished to be there could just turn up, as it was a public place.

Matthew stood beside me, waiting anxiously until my phone call was over, asking if we were going to go. I asked him if he thought we should go, and he became excited at the prospect of actually going to the beach at night and said, "Yes, Mum. Please, can we go? Can we go, please?"

"Okay, let's go," I responded as I bent over and kissed him on the forehead. We gathered together a blanket, pillow, my handbag, and some warm clothes for Matt, and off we headed to Bronte Beach. I do love spontaneity.

We arrived at Bronte Beach and found a great car park, nice and close to the beach itself. Crossing the road, we looked around for a good spot, close to the action. We found one at the outer edge of a circle made up of giant chunks of various crystals and sat down. Singing and chanting rang out in echoes over the beach fore-shores. Matthew and I found ourselves sitting at the outside the large circle, with my foot actually touching one of the rose quartz crystals, while around the other side was a group of people who obviously not only knew each other, but knew all the words to the songs, along with the full meaning of what the celebrations were all about. Having never heard these singing chants before, I found by the end of the night we knew the words off by heart.

The air was filled with the wafting smells of incense, campfire smoke, tobacco, and sausage sizzles. People were gathering around this central, circular focal point. Some were sitting inside, while Matthew and I and others sat around the outside of the crystal circle. My pillow came in handy, softening the bumpy, uneven, dusty earth beneath us, through which sprigs of grass tried to unsuccessfully sprout through. My legs were crossed, with one of my feet touching a giant crystal, while Matthew chose to sit on my crossed legs on his pillow. I was amazed to realize that we actually got a front row seat slap-bang in the centre of the all the celebrations. Matthew was quite content to sit inside my crossed legs, leaning back against me, listening to the songs, and watching all the strange hippy types coming and going. He was a well-behaved little boy. I was proud of him.

We watched and listened to the chanting and singing until we slowly caught onto the words, enabling us to join in. As Matthew's normal bed time came and went, he slowly drifted off to sleep on my knee.

When 10:30 p.m. arrived, the time the planets were predicted to align, the most uncanny cloud formation occurred above our heads. The clouds spiraled into what looked like a central vortex directly above the chanting circle. I don't know if this was what was expected, but it formed, much to everyone's excitement and disbelief. This cloud formation coincided with the time the actual planets aligned, even though we could not see the planets at all, due to the clouds that were forming overhead.

Hands were pointing upward in awe as this magical cloud formation and natural phenomenon developed. Matthew and I were in the midst of it, even though he was fast asleep. There were hundreds of people on the beach and grassy areas—from babes in strollers to the elderly enjoying the festivities and party-like environment and the mildness of the evening. Most were there just to be a part of a celebration, knowing very little (if anything at all) about the convergence side of it. I would have fallen into that category of being ignorant of the true meaning of the words harmonic convergence. I only found out about this planetary alignment that evening because of Matthew hearing it on the news.

Following the end of the festivities, I struggled, but managed all the same, to get up and carry all our stuff—including Matthew, who was fast asleep in my arms. We finally made it across the grassy beach front, up onto the footpath, and across the road to where my car was parked. As I was driving home, I pondered whether our being there was possibly meant to change us, or for that matter, even make us feel any different in our day-to-day lives. I questioned a lot of things in my mind on our homeward drive from Bronte that night.

When I think back, that was a notable turning point in my life, where I was drawn toward spiritual things and deeper understandings. Did it change my life? Who really knows? I tend to think it may have, but it was a nice night out that drew my attention toward those little feelings that yearn for deeper meaning and understanding.

For me, I felt it drew my attention toward a spiritual path or back onto one. When life tends to pull one off track, something usually happens to bring us back again, and they are usually the choices we make. From that point onward, through my own efforts, things certainly began to change in many different ways.

As it says in the Bible, "so I say unto you: ask and it will be given to you; seek and you shall find; knock and the door will be opened to you" (Luke 11:9, NIV). This is very true. In normal, everyday words, it simply means that you can do what you want or dream—go for it; it will come. It is not an empty statement. In other words, follow your dreams, aim high and go for it, believe in miracles, and ask for what you truly want—but be careful what you ask for; you might just get it.

CHAPTER FIFTEEN

Coffs Harbour—
Thirty-nine Years of Age

In 1990, while living in our own home in Coffs Harbour with my son, Matthew, I awoke spontaneously in the early hours of the morning in absolute agony. It seemed so far removed from the condition I went to sleep in. My throat was so painful that the saliva began trickling out of the sides of my mouth, and try as I might, I could not swallow. I had previously been a sufferer of strep throats for a good part of my younger life until 1979. I sacrificed a holiday cruise with my friends Sandy, Marilyn, Amanda, and Elle during my nursing training to instead have a tonsillectomy. I preferred to take time out of my holidays rather than out of my work time, as I had never used any sick leave, being a usually healthy young woman. I intended to nurse in third world countries once I had graduated, and with the amount of sore throats I had been getting, I decided it was a safer option to get them removed in Australia instead of from a makeshift hospital tent somewhere in a grief-stricken part of the world with less-trained staff and no hygiene or running water.

My hospitalization did not run smoothly, either. I was a dreadful patient, falsifying my fluid balance charts because I just couldn't swallow, so I wrote on the charts I had been drinking good amounts of fluids and voiding equal amounts. Upon arriving home following my discharge (mind you, I signed myself out), I became very unwell with a huge post-op throat infection. In the middle of the night, I found myself rolling around on the dewy grass to help bring my soaring temperature down. This was gradually corrected with liquid antibiotics prescribed from a friend, Doctor Jim. It all ended well and with a lovely weight loss of twenty kilograms, because I hadn't been able to eat for nearly six weeks. It all ended up fine in the end. From that point onward, I had never suffered from a sore throat until this night in 1990. It was a mind-bender and something right out of the ballpark. Having gone to bed completely normal and healthy without a hint of a sore throat and waking up just a few hours later in absolute agony, crying in pain while clutching my throat and seizing a torch from my top bedside drawer, I made my way to the bathroom to see if I could find what was causing me so much pain. I wanted to see if there were any red areas, swelling, or white spots (pus) in the back of my throat, which would have meant I had a throat infection. All I saw was blood-tinged saliva coming from no apparent area. There was no pus, no temperature, no redness, and no hint that anything was wrong—apart, of course, from the pain.

As I leaned over the sink to look at my throat in the mirror, some type of answer for the agonizing pain I was experiencing was intuited to me. The telepathic intuitive language that I knew so well began to come through loud and clear. It went something like, "You have woken too soon; nothing you do will help. But if you return to sleep immediately, you will wake up with no pain or discomfort at all. You simply woke too soon; return to sleep now." I couldn't stop sobbing. The pain was horrific and excruciating; it was as if I had my tonsils ripped out of my throat with a jagged, rusty knife with no anaesthetic. I couldn't even brush my teeth. So I returned to bed in tears, holding a face cloth at my mouth to prevent me from dribbling (because I couldn't swallow). I couldn't even swallow water. Trying to rinse my mouth had me making a mess everywhere, so I gave up and returned to my bed.

Waking up at the crack of dawn the following morning, I observed a tinge of blood on my pillow case, which made me realize that my pain I had experienced in the middle of the night was not a dream.

Gingerly swallowing, poking my tongue out, clearing my throat, and swallowing repeatedly, there was no pain whatsoever. I remembered getting up the previous night. The torch was still in the bathroom, so I knew it wasn't a dream, and with the blood tinge on my pillow case, I knew I wasn't imagining what happened in the early hours of that morning.

I could still recall the telepathic message telling me I had woken too soon, and if I returned to sleep as instructed, the pain would no longer be there when I awoke the next morning. I knew then that I had been abducted by my alien friends the night before, but I had no recall whatsoever about being transported—or, for that matter, even seeing them. Without a doubt, I knew what part of my body they had been working on.

With the pain I had experienced earlier that morning and the lack of it now, there was indeed something strange going on—but as usual, I didn't tell a soul. By the time morning came, I had woken to a completely healed and quite normal throat; therefore, seeing a doctor would do no good whatsoever, because he wouldn't see anything anyway. It was about a week or so later that I awoke one morning to find a very small, silver, shiny metallic disc in my bed. It resembled an old 45 music record. There was a black dot just off the centre, and it was the size of the pad of my little finger. I put it away in my drawer and didn't look at it again, but I did take a photo of it.

What was strange was that two or three years before finding the disc in my bed, while living in Dee Why, NSW and suffering a sore neck, I had been referred for an x-ray which was taken of my cervical spine and a good portion of my skull. That disc was seen quite clearly in my occipital bone at the base of my skull. The technician explained it away by saying it was something on the table I was laying on. The subject was never broached again. Isn't funny how things can be so easily swept under the carpet without a second thought? It was like nothing really mattered, nor should it be investigated, discussed, or talked about—in fact, it should be forgotten or left by the wayside in pure disinterest. This is a typical result of an abduction or visitation.

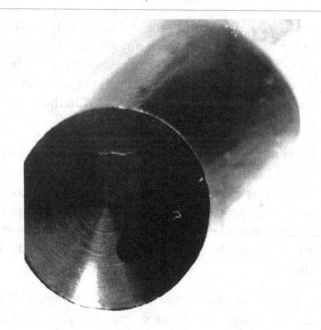

Pam, a long-term friend of mine from Coffs Harbour who is a qualified hypnotherapist, after hearing my thoughts regarding abductions, aliens, and UFOs, offered to regress me and take me back in time to either prove or disprove my assumptions about abductions that she felt may have been buried in my past. After the appointment was made, a week or so later, I arrived at her home, and she took me to her clinic.

I lay on a couch in her little semi-detached clinic while she sat in an arm chair beside me, but slightly out of my peripheral vision. Gentle music played in the background while Pam's voice guided me through a deep relaxation process, landing me back into the past—way, way back into the past. Memories were stirred as I uttered words of abduction, reliving the situation from a two- and then a four-year-old's perspective. Pam moved me forward in twenty-minute increments, thereby giving me an understanding of what was going on, although the abduction process was disjointed and not free-flowing. It didn't seem to make any sense to me because of the twenty-minute gaps between.

I woke from the regression feeling invigorated, but the memory of the abduction only allowed me to recall disjointed portions, which was a little confusing. It was similar to a door from the past being flung open for me to see what was inside, but I ended up in each room, not knowing how I got there or who the people were. I feel Pam was successful at taking me back to my childhood, letting me realize I was abducted, and allowing me the satisfaction of knowing I was not altogether crazy for having thoughts of abduction. However, her method gave me an inconsistent recall—but at least I knew it was real.

I went home amazed by the experience, feeling confident that I had been in contact with ETs, but not really feeling the continuity of events, which I felt should have given me a more fluent flow of events. Instead, I got one that didn't fully make sense.

CHAPTER SIXTEEN

UFO Probes/Spheres—1990,
Coffs Harbour

Sometime during the winter months of 1990, two friends (mother and daughter) came over for an evening of guided meditation, followed by supper and a lovely catch-up chat that we girls love so much. We had been friends since my initial move to Coffs Harbour. Following our meditation that night, we openly discussed our inward journeys and shared notes, so to speak, on what we got from the meditation. Our conversation then took a turn toward UFOs and other spiritual matters. This subject is close to my heart, as it was with the girls. After talking about the subject for a while, it was no surprise what happened next.

Connie made a move to depart, as it was getting late, so we all stood and gave each other a hug good night. At this time, I don't think it was far after 9:00 p.m. Opening the front door while still chatting, we all walked down the driveway in the cool of the night air toward the road, where their car was parked.

It was a nice, fresh, clear night, with a bit of a nip in the air. We still had things to talk about, so we stopped halfway down the driveway, where my duplex ended and the front yard began. We were a little more sheltered from the night breeze on the corner of the building. Connie and her daughter, Kay, obviously saw something behind me, and as I continued talking, their eyes were stuck fast on something above and behind me. My attention was drawn to follow their gaze to see what they were so obviously gob smacked by. There in plain sight, a slowly descending ball from the sky made its way straight down to stop about eye level from me. The girls looked mesmerized, with mouths half-opened, staring at it, not listening to a word I was talking about. To tell the truth, I couldn't remember what I was talking about either when I saw it. It stopped dead-still about four feet away from me at eye level. I could see very clearly a small, round, clear, white sphere that was a little bigger than a golf ball but not quite as big as a tennis ball. It was not a bug; it had no wings, no buzz, made no noise at all and didn't move at all—not even with the breeze and sudden gusts of wind.

In the middle of the sphere was a pink-orange color that expanded and pulsated like a heartbeat. With each beat, this color seemed to take over the white sphere that it was. We all confirmed to each other what we were all seeing, and yes, we were all seeing the same thing. Connie and her daughter, Kay, stood on the driveway, staring in amazement and shock—in fact, Connie looked petrified. I, however, stepped onto the lawn in the front of my home with about three to four feet between it and myself and slowly approached it with my hand outstretched, palm facing up, as if I was calling a dog or a bird, even talking to it, saying, "It's okay. I'm not going to hurt you. Come on, come to me."

As I was doing this, I was pondering the thought of it being a glow worm or a flying bug, but I had never seen a glowing white sphere with a pulsating heartbeat before. Also, I noticed that it didn't have feelers, limbs, or wings, nor did it have any type of body shape. It was a sphere—a ball shape. To me, it seemed to be a living thing; it had an awareness of where we were and what we were doing. It most certainly didn't want to be touched or approached, so to me, it was alive. It was watching us, studying us, but wouldn't let us come too close.

I continued to walk slowly toward it with my hand outstretched, but as soon as I got close to it, it zoomed about twenty feet east, straight across to my neighbor's front yard, and just stopped in midair, as if it was scared of us, taunting us, or playing with us while remaining about three to four feet off the ground, motionless. It was as if it knew exactly what it was doing. It was alive. It was toying with us, playing cat and mouse. The girls remained together on the driveway, huddled in fear and disbelief where they were initially, reluctant to move in any direction, just watching what I was doing.

I walked across my driveway, down the embankment, across the neighbors' driveway, and onto their front lawn until I was once again within a few feet from it, as close as I got before. It shot back to my place, and so I returned to the girls, asking if they had been watching all of this. They silently nodded incessantly. Both of them stood beside each other, looking on, but acting very unnerved. It just hovered in front of us, observing our movements carefully in protection of itself (or recording our thoughts or movements—who knows?). Then, slowly, it started rising, with its reddish-orange centre beating like a heart.

It rose up and up for about eight to ten minutes without darting off or deviating to the left or right until it disappeared into the darkness of the night, heading straight upward. Please, someone tell me if a bug or floating plant moves in this way while maintaining a straight line and stance in the middle of the air without the slightest movement? This was something not of our world, and I felt blessed to have seen it, but disappointed it didn't allow me to touch it or communicate in some way with it, God knows, I would never have hurt it.

Very shortly after this, we said our goodnights, and the girls departed and went on their merry way home. The strange thing about this little encounter is that we had all been friends for quite a while, taking a keen interest in psychic phenomena and spiritual things—UFOs and such—but not one of us discussed this event or even felt compelled to talk about it again. It wasn't wiped from our thoughts or our memories, but we simply never had the inclination again to discuss it. How weird is that? Later I found out from books that this little sphere is called a probe. Probes are seen by others from different areas of the world. It is surmised that it is indeed a small apparatus sent from a craft to record thoughts and subconscious feelings—things at the time I didn't know anything about. Until that time, I had never heard of one, seen one, or even knew about them. I believe they are a sort of recording device, but goodness knows whether it was recording our thoughts, our conversations, or our attempts to try to talk to it. We will never know exactly what it was doing or what the results were, but sure as eggs, it was definitely not of this world. Did we report it? No—who on earth would we report to? It continues to amaze me that the wondrous things I have been witness to in my life didn't seem to be a topic of conversation. None of them were forgotten; they were just never discussed. It's this lack of interest on a dynamic topic that makes me believe that these suppressed conversations were brought about by our alien friends, because the time for discussion was not for then. Maybe it's all for now?

Chapter Seventeen

Abduction Confirmation— John Haige, 1991

It was some time during 1989 that I purchased a book from my favorite bookstore in Coffs Harbour, but I didn't get to read it until 1991. It was written by a local author, John Haigh, who wrote on channelled information from an ancient extraterrestrial source, Eldermos. The book in question was *Serving Planet Earth.*

At that particular time in my life, I was writing children's short stories, but I had also kept some beautiful inspirational poetry I had written from 1978. These inspirations came at a time in my life when I was doing my nurse's training at Manly District Hospital—at the time when Elvis died, bush fires were burning in the Warringah area, and exam nerves were upon us. Life was exciting.

I would spontaneously wake in the night between 1:00 and 3:00 in the morning and write rhyming words in verse, then return to sleep again. After writing dozens of these verses, all of which had morals to their stories, I eventually plucked up the courage to read them to friends, who encouraged me to publish. I toyed with the idea, although I had no idea whatsoever as to how to go about publishing or even how to find a publisher (this was long before computers were in every house).

I decided to try and contact the author of the book I'd just finished reading after reading in the book jacket that he lived locally in Bellingen, just a short forty-five-minute drive away. I sourced his phone number from the local phone book and let my fingers do the walking. It all seemed so easy.

The phone started ringing. He picked up and answered, introducing himself as John Haige. Following suit, I also introduced myself, stating I had bought and just finished reading his book, congratulating him on the content. I then went on to tell him about my own attempts at putting my intuited poetry into a book and that I would really value his input and guidance as to how to publish, where to go, and how to go about publishing them.

There was a pause in conversation—a long, pregnant pause, followed by a request for my address. He spoke quietly and deliberately when he asked, "What was your name again?" Then he continued, "I shall be at your place shortly, Judy."

What followed was (another) one of the most mind-blowing experiences of my entire life.

Approximately an hour later, there came a few knocks at my front door, and there stood John Haige. He was a tall man, dressed in a crisp white shirt, blue jeans, and a jacket. He had whitish-grey, shoulder-length hair and a matching long beard in the same natural silvery-white colour. He was a very well-groomed gentleman. His eyes were a piercingly beautiful blue, yet he appeared amazingly young for the grey-white hair he possessed. When he spoke, his voice was quiet and unassuming. He seemed like a very gentle man.

I invited him to enter my home and led him into my lounge room, where we both took seats facing each other on two-seater lounge seats, giving us comfort while assuming a proper and respectable distance from one another.

The initial reason for John's visit turned out to have nothing whatsoever to do with the end result. There were no discussions whatsoever at any time about my book, my writings, or anything to do with publishing. This meeting was a very obvious predestined appointment to give me a positive confirmation of my UFO encounters and abductions while giving me the information that I was somehow meant to hear. We had not discussed anything to do with UFOs—nor, for that matter, anything about myself whatsoever—previous to our phone call just an hour before. We did not know each other prior to his arrival at my front door. Everything you are about to read about came as a bit of a shock and a revelation. His book was a channelled book by a supposed extraterrestrial, so what transpired during his visit turned out to be quite miraculous, uncanny, and very surreal—something out of the twilight zone. It was loaded with confirmation and information that I was evidently supposed to receive.

After introductions, a short conversation, and pleasantries took place, I stood and offered him a cup of tea or coffee, to which he responded humbly, "A glass of water would be nice, thank you." He then went on to explain that he had never offered to do this with a virtual stranger before and that it was not a party trick, but in my case, he felt there was some type of confirmation I needed, but he didn't know in regard to what, exactly, at this stage.

John explained that with my permission, he would take himself into a self-induced deep meditative state to allow a wise and ancient soul to communicate with me through his body. He added that he had no idea why, after meeting me for a completely different reason, he felt compelled to do this. We both agreed that this kind of spontaneity always has a reason behind it, and so both of us agreed it would be a good idea to go ahead and enable this wise soul (supposedly an extraterrestrial source who spoke throughout the book I had just finished reading) to talk directly to me.

John advised me that during the next hour or so, he would not be present, but instead would leave his body to allow this specific ancient disembodied spirit entity to use his body as if it were his own. I was also advised strongly that under no circumstances was I to touch him. Regardless of what he may sound or look like, he would be taken care of completely; therefore, any interference by touch from me was definitely not permitted. I agreed.

After confirming with me the above and following my nervous but excited nod of approval, he settled comfortably back into the lounge chair, took a few deep breaths, and slowly went into a deep, meditative state, which to me looked like he was drifting off to sleep.

There I sat in my chair, directly opposite him, nervously watching intently for any signs of trickery or strangeness. Ten minutes went by, with me now shifting my gaze to the clock, the walls, the curtains, out through the windows, and back again to his face. This was all a little strange and surreal, making me feel somewhat uncomfortable and maybe even a little scared. I felt quite alone, sitting in my lounge room with a supposedly empty body sitting opposite me, void of a soul, with an expected stranger about to jump in to talk with me. Come on—anyone would feel a little apprehensive, a little scared, and well out of their comfort zone.

All of sudden, John's body leaned forward. He gave a slight clearing of the throat, and still with his eyes closed, he spoke, introducing himself as Eldamos. He went on to say, "It is an honor to meet with you, Judy."

I felt embarrassed by the extent of his warm wishes and responded verbally back to him, "Oh, no. The honor is mine." He continued with a discourse that floored me.

"Judy, the honor is mine, and I say this because you have no idea who you truly are." By now, I was feeling very uneasy, because I knew who I was, and I felt that he had me confused with someone else. He continued, "You do realize that since you were a small baby, you have been in constant contact throughout your life with aliens?"

I gasped in horror, because I knew I had been with them—but how did he know? He then stated, "I feel we have a revelation here?" He continued, "You have in fact been abducted throughout your life approximately every two years. Were you aware of this, Judy?"

"Well, yes, I knew that I had been abducted, but didn't realize it was *every* two years," I replied in shock. My mind was then going ten to the dozen. How did he know this? I suddenly recalled that Pam had only just hypnotized me a week or two ago and said something similar, which I thought was a little strange, but believable. Now this ancient dead man in another man's body was confirming the very same thing! Wow—my God. I was overwhelmed and shocked. I then brazenly asked, "Why would they want me every two years for? And who am I that you honor me, and that you say I don't know who I truly am?"

John's face gave a slight twist that remotely resembled a smile as he went on to say, "I can only answer half of that question, because the other half requires permission." He continued to tell me that the abductions over the years of my life may appear to the multitudes to be invasive, although previous consent had been obtained. Their intent was to make those of us who had been abducted better people, to be used as an example of how they cope with life, experiences, pain, anger, rejection, stress, and all manner of things that to most would appear a hard life and too difficult to handle.

He told me that most abductees are implanted with genetically changed and other invisible implants that offer special gifts along the lines of kindness, compassion, understanding, clairvoyance, clairaudience, healing abilities, being able to read people's feelings, telepathy, artistic and creative inclination, and a growing closeness to the God within. It was true; I did possess those things. He said that my communication with God, as we choose to call him, would soon become so profound that it would be as if I was talking with him on the telephone or I would be able to journal a conversation with him with no doubts between my thoughts and his answers.

"Wow, unbelievable. That would be so wonderful. I hope you are right," I said in awe. (This did eventuate some years later in my life— in 1998—and still does.) I told him that I didn't practice or use those gifts anymore and wasn't even sure if I still had them, even though I knew they were within me. He reminded me that they are there, regardless of practice or use, and that when needed or reminded about them, they would come to the fore. I then timidly inquired, "You said you honored me. Is this a normal greeting for you to say to people you meet? And what did you mean when you said I don't realize who I am? Who am I?"

He nodded and responded, "To answer this question, I must firstly ask permission from those higher than both of us to reveal this to you. Could you wait?"

"Yes, of course," I responded eagerly. So there I sat. A good ten to fifteen minutes must have passed before his body began to move and that familiar throat-clearing began happening again in order to allow the spirit to gain control of John's voice box so he could talk.

It was a little scary, sitting in a room, seemingly alone, waiting for a supposed wise sage who was not of this world to enter into John's body. It was a very strange and surreal feeling, one that I felt quite honored to be part of. Following a little movement, a jerk here and there, and a little throat-clearing, he returned.

He said he had been given permission to reveal who I was. Here I was, sitting and waiting for his verbal discourse to reveal to me who I was. Hullo? I knew who I was, but who else was I? Or worse still, who did he believe I was?

This was crazy, confusing, and exciting, yet I was hanging off his every word. He began by telling me that he had met with several entities which were closely related to me through many lifetimes—my guidance, protectors, guardians, and others who were of the opinion that at this juncture in my life, I could handle the information that was about to be given to me without it changing my life, my inner being, or my future.

He began, "There is a hierarchy of individuals from varying planets in the cosmos, as well as different galaxies in the universe, regardless of whether the inhabitants of planet Earth recognizes this or not. The human race believes there is no life on any other planets simply because their means of discovering it is not capable of delivering the truth, although they feel that their equipment, due to its cost, would collect this data if there were anyone else out there. There is so much life out there of varying kinds, but human beings have no idea how to find and recognize it. You, as a race, may have equipment and technology, but your knowledge is limited, regardless of how advanced you think you are. Where humans are concerned, they are of the belief, 'I'll believe it when I see it' and 'If our technology cannot pick it up, then it does not exist.' Both of these are grossly incorrect."

He continued without a word of interruption from me, "This has nothing to do with the true reality of existence. While mankind's ignorance continues with their desire to rule and dominate, they will not advance in the areas they must know. To go forth in ignorance is dangerous; therefore, they will be watched, and some of their interplanetary travel will be curtailed and show itself as glitches, mistakes, and accidents until he is mature and learned enough to venture to outer space unsupervised. This cannot and will not be tolerated for the safety of all concerned. You—the human race—are watched constantly as a mother watches her children, because as a race, you cannot be trusted to take care of the planet that was entrusted to you. Your irresponsibility is too great.

"It is seen that not only are you raping your own planet of what keeps it whole, complete, and intact and in existence, but you are also fighting and killing each other for greed, domination, and worse, aggression, under the name of your religions, which is both barbaric and completely incorrect. But still, over eons of time, you have not grown up. Now your intent is to source commodities under the name of discovery from distant planetary sources for greed, ego, and competitiveness with other countries on your own planet—ownership and dominance. Human beings are very competitive and dangerous, where life, you believe, is your right to dominate, control, annihilate, experiment with, and destroy. There is very little advancement since human life first began on your planet. You can no longer be trusted, because you still have not proven yourselves as being peace-loving human beings.

"There is a gathering of beings representative of all planetary systems in the universe, and at times, they meet to make major decisions and changes for the benefit of the entire universe, cosmos, including mankind on earth. This has been ongoing throughout history, just as your earthly representatives meet to discuss matters of importance concerning your world. These you call summits. Our interplanetary gatherings work on a larger scale for more pressing reasons with the entire cosmos, including the planet Earth.

"For example, if planet Earth's occupants place their planet or other planets at risk, this will automatically affect all solar systems, planets, and space due to the gravitational pull one has on the other; hence, we are all connected, and human beings still do not understand or realize this. Therefore, if one planet is destroyed, they will all be affected, and this will put the entire cosmos at risk. With this in mind, we must step in to protect it. We cannot allow its destruction. For in the destruction of Earth, so the destruction of other planets will be affected, as a chain reaction. Therefore, in some cases, you cannot be permitted to leave Earth, as you will recognize by some of your aborted attempts to leave your planet.

"It is better to eradicate the human race than allow the destruction of the planet for the sake of the entire universe. It is for these reasons we would interfere. Your greatest sightings of us are when catastrophes are about to happen or shortly after them. Our reasons for being in your earth space is not to harm, but to give you experiences that will help you to evolve, among many other reasons.

"Humans believe that if they plant a flag in the ground, then that land or planet is theirs, hence ownership. There are no owners. Planets— any planet is not owned; it is gifted to its inhabitants to care-take once they have been declared by this counsel to be worthy of it. Any inhabitant of a planet has to prove their capability to care for it and appreciate it while having these same qualities toward their own peoples, but the human race seems to threaten not only themselves with extinction if the dominating party is not recognized or obeyed, but the entire planet, and unbeknown to you, the domino effect on the cosmos.

"We are after a more peaceful, loving, and beneficial outcome, not one made by brute force and threats of distinction. It is frightful to see differing cultures fighting for ownership of land that will never be theirs or the riches that this land produces in its core. They are willing to kill and be killed for something that was given to you all to share and prosper from together. Each of your major countries have weapons capable of not only massive destruction of your lands, but the cessation of life—any life as you know it. Surely you can very plainly recognize not only the selfishness of such weapons, but proof you are not yet ready to sit at the table with us to negotiate planetary and earthly outcomes?

"These meetings cover topics such as water, soil sampling, invasions, atomic and volatile threatening substances that can contaminate land, weapons in outer space, atmospheric pollutants, natural disasters, and the effects these things can have upon the universal planetary systems. We monitor life in its totality and take samples when needed for future growth. This you will not and do not understand right now, but very soon, we will be talking together—but you are not ready right now."

He went on to say that there were six representatives from the planet Earth who attended these meetings, and that I was one of them. "No," I responded in utter shock and disbelief, "surely not. I have been an air hostess who constantly suffered air-sickness, and not only that, but ever since I was a small child, any motion made me sick, because my ear balance is right out of whack. Why would they want someone with such bad ear balance?"

I prattled on stupidly, being embarrassed by such a huge honor, exposing the idiocy of myself through nervousness. John's face smiled, and he continued, "It's not the physicality of the body, but what you bring to these meetings—your knowledge, your lives of experience, your attitude, your desire for peaceful, compassionate, and productive outcomes. These individuals who represent Earth are not your head politicians; they are not the famous or the well-known. They are human beings who possess the necessary qualities and knowledge of prolonging, peaceful, and satisfying existences."

He calmly nodded, smiled, and continued gently, "Your body matter is changed and adjusted to adapt to a different environment, and this enables you to travel intergalacticly virtually instantly. You have been attending these summits for many lives, not just this one; it's a continuation. The human body cannot be damaged. Your memories of star patterns and the affinity you have with the stars, space, and moon cycles are hints of you being there before while being educated from a level far deeper than you would realize. You have a familiarity, but don't remember, as it played out. You also have the ability to communicate using telepathy with those onboard UFOs. This is how and why you can sense the species you know within Earth's atmosphere." He continued to tell me, "We trust there will be no changes in your attitude now you are aware of this? It was kept from you for your own protection, because it would be very difficult for any human being to learn who they truly are and what they are capable of doing while believing you are a human being, living an everyday human existence, not realizing the importance of your input regarding intergalactic meetings as a representative of planet Earth."

I responded with enthusiasm and exuberant excitement, "No, you can trust me that none of this information will change me in any way. If I have managed to do both jobs while being ignorant, then I will make every effort not to let this information interfere with my attitude." I went on to say, "I really want to believe you, but find it very difficult to accept that I am someone of importance, while being me, but am also honored to serve our planet in this way, and honored that it was felt by those you consulted that I was ready to be given this information. Who am I to be chosen to do the job of representing planet Earth?"

He responded, with a smile, "It is not who you are here and now, but all that you have been, and the qualities and attitudes you possess, and what you have brought with you to each and every incarnation since your beginning. It is the very soul of you that has accumulated the knowledge that is sought by those at these meetings, and this is who we honor." His response was cool and calm. "You now have sufficient information to assimilate at this time, and you will grow in time to understand where you in fact came from. When you write a book in the future, we suggest that further information will only cause concern, and this is not the desired effect."

"Me, write a book?" I asked. "I don't think so. Who would be interested in reading a book on extraterrestrials and UFOs, a subject that no one can really prove or understand? This is quite ridiculous, and I don't know enough to write on it or to fill a book." He smiled and nodded and said no more.

The spirit entity, Eldamos, bowed and said farewell. He added that he wanted to prevent any adverse effects on John, due to the length of time that he had been absent from his body. A few minutes went by, and all of a sudden, John returned to himself, where Eldamos had dwelt for the past hour or so. Time just flew by; it only felt like a minute or two. All I knew was that my mind was swimming with all this astounding information. No one, not even John himself, was there to hear or witness it; this was purely for my ears only. Did I really believe it? It was all just so overwhelming and unbelievable, but oh, so wonderful.

To tell anyone this would sound conceited and would appear that I was experiencing visions of grandeur, which are sure signs of psychotic behavior. This would prove to most anyone that I was a sick puppy, which I know I am not. I kept this meeting secret until these very words were printed on this page, over two decades after the event.

Needless to say, John Haigh left my home shortly after he woke up, never to return or contact me again. His purpose was to confirm my abductions throughout my life and give me confirmation that what I had previously been shown through my hypnotism just the week before with Pam was true. No one could dream up or arrange such coincidences.

We didn't even discuss my children's books or poetry at all; they didn't even warrant a mention. That was obviously not the reason he was meant to be in my home at all. God works in mysterious ways. I obviously needed to be given this information, and the source of this information (not of this world) was brought about in a very strange way—right to my very doorstep from millions of light years away. And here is the book that was predicted. Can you believe it?

CHAPTER EIGHTEEN

Witnessing a UFO—Coffs Harbour, 1991

Some months later, in 1991, while still living in Coffs Harbour with my son, I had a girlfriend over for dinner, and we decided to do what my son and I enjoyed doing on nice, clear evenings. One of and my favorite after-dinner nighttime treats was to gather together bean bags, quilts, and pillows. Shortly after dark, we would sneak out onto the driveway, where the warmth of the daytime sun still remained in the concrete. We loved to lay outside and watch the night sky, often times seeing satellites pass over head, travelling in different directions, and the odd shooting star catapulting through the heavens. We were very seldom disappointed by movement in the skies.

Matthew was eight years old, and he and I would snuggle up together under the quilt while competing to see who would see the next shooting star or satellite. I had an elderly neighbour who had more of a social life than I could ever dream of. She and I owned our duplexes; therefore, we both had access to the same driveway. Somehow, Matthew and I avoided being sprung when lying on the driveway at night. I guess that was half the fun and excitement, never getting caught, but it was fun all the same. How does one explain away sitting in the middle of the driveway, staring at the sky, on a bean bag?

Sometimes my neighbour would arrive home in her car as Matthew and I were enjoying our own private night sky viewing. All of a sudden, we would get the initial tell-tale headlight beam shining up the driveway before her car actually appeared. This gave us enough time, if we moved quickly, to grab everything, throw it in through the front door, and dive onto it in the lounge room, laughing and squealing in delight, like kids, often times bruising ourselves doing it. Those are the wonderful memories of doing crazy things that are great to look back upon. Those memories make me smile.

But on this particular night, my friend Kerrie was a guest at our dinner table. Following our evening meal, she said she would love to join Matthew and I out on the driveway with our night sky. She said it sounded like a fun and relaxing thing to do after dinner, so she accepted the offer to join us. We didn't expect my neighbor's grandchildren to be home, and so within minutes of us settling in to our positions on the driveway a short distance from my garage, they too brought their quilts out and huddled up with us without any invitation. They said they wanted to star gaze with us, so we all huddled up like a bunch of kids together in a long row on the path. It was a gloriously clear night, with only the odd few large, puffy, "mashed potato" clouds hanging around. We lay watching the night sky in our little group of seven, giggling and talking.

We were definitely not disappointed. Within the hour, something mind-blowing happened, much to our shock and excitement. It was something I dreamed of seeing, but never in a million years expected to see, especially on my driveway with a group of giggling kids.

Overhead, a massive under-belly of a huge craft appeared, travelling north to south. It was moving very slowly and absolutely silently overhead. It was so close we could see the chunks of metal on the under carriage. There were no lights visible from inside or outside of the craft at all. From our driveway position, we could just see the silhouette from the clear sky behind it. It was a massive circular shape. We couldn't see the top of it at all, and the circumference spanned about ten blocks. It was gigantic and low enough to have it move overhead for some minutes before the end passed over. It looked like a mother-ship.

As it passed overhead, it disappeared into some clouds (the only clouds that could be seen) that seemed to accumulate in a southerly direction. It just appeared to evaporate into thin air. We all waited for it to come out the other side of the clouds, but sadly, we are still waiting. As it was going over head, one of the neighbor's children yelled out, "Look, look," pointing upward. "Can you see it? Can you see it?"

All of us echoed out loudly, "Yes," hanging on to each other in utter silence. It came and went without a word out of any of us. Even the small kids weren't frightened, but they did snuggle in to who they were laying next to. None of us panicked. "What can you see?" someone asked, just to check that we were all seeing the same thing. Following our confirmation that we were indeed all seeing the same thing, we lay there in silence, just watching this massive UFO move slowly over head till it disappeared. It was a thousand times bigger than any of our jumbo jets, and it was very low in the sky, but well above our houses and the mountain that stood behind us in Coffs Harbour.

The strangest thing about all seven of us seeing this UFO was the silence of the craft. Once it passed, we all got up, took our respective quilts and pillows, said goodnight, and went to our homes. The weirdest thing (that seemed usual for any sightings that I have ever witnessed) was that from that day onward, nothing was ever spoken about it again. Even the children didn't tell their grandmother (my neighbour). I always remembered it, and when discussing it with Kerrie years later, she too remembered it, but never felt compelled to talk about it. None of the kids next door, Matthew, or me ever discussed it. This is so strange for something of such extreme, monumental importance. This is the uncanny thing with UFO;, it's not that it's wiped from the memory so much as it's met with ambivalence.

This is the sort of thing that you will see throughout this book—the same words of complacency. That is why the subject isn't talked about. That's why not many people report them. They don't know who to ring or how would this be received. Once the police are informed, it doesn't go anywhere, and when news rooms get a story of a sighting, they sensationalize them, making everyone reading about it think it's a big joke. The person reporting it is made to look like an idiot when at the end of the show, the compere rolls their eyes, dictating their silent opinion of the event. Who wants open ridicule like this?

Chapter Nineteen

A Current Affair with Budd Hopkins, 1992

In 1992, while working as a part-time registered nurse and pre-natal educator in Coffs Harbour, I also worked at various pharmacies as a baby health nurse and registered nurse and shop assistant one day a week in each pharmacy up and down the coast, travelling to Woolgoolga one day, Coffs Harbour another, Bellingen another, and down south as far as Nambucca Heads for yet another day. This offered me a close to full week of work. It was actually a wonderful driving experience each day and a lovely time of my life.

At the same time, I spent my evenings doing a baby problem column for a local magazine and teaching my own privately run prenatal and postnatal classes at Opal Cove function rooms one day a week. My life was full of variation. My son, Matthew, also joined me as part of that happy picture. I had lots of quality time with him, like going fishing, going to dinner at least once a week, movies, walks, and visiting friends, and at night, lying on the driveway, drinking in the night sky together or sitting on my front porch on the two-seater winging chair, having deep and meaningful talks together. Being a good mother was very important to me, and I loved every minute of it.

I especially loved my Fridays at the lovely Bellingen Chemist shop in the centre of the main street of Bellingen. It took approximately forty-five minutes driving time in a southerly direction from Coffs Harbour, where I lived at the time. Each week, the glorious drive felt like a trip into another world. Basically, Bellingen was out in the country, where one steps back in time to another century with fresh air and farm smells that waft through the car window. I found my Fridays a really pleasant experience. Perhaps this is because I'm a Taurus. The natural smell of cow dung and freshly cut grass makes me feel at home, while giving me a gentle reminder that nature, in its purest sense, makes one feel at home.

Upon arrival at the chemist shop, I would begin setting up to receive all the local babies, answer mothercraft questions, perform baby weighs, check breast feeding, take blood pressure, and offer counseling in all areas as part of my position as the town's baby nurse and registered nurse. In addition to the day time treks up and down the coast, I had a position as a prenatal educator at a private hospital in the maternity area, being a midwife and RN.

During one of these weekly sojourns, I was driving toward Bellingen; listening to my music tapes; and experiencing that lovely, contented, blissful feeling. All of a sudden, I heard that old, familiar telepathy begin—that familiar sense of recognizing the language I'd been taught since childhood and a knowledge that there were UFOs somewhere in our skies. Try as I might, I could not see anything out of my car window remotely resembling a UFO. It was bright and sunny, which gave me less chance of seeing anything, but nevertheless, I studied the expansive sky for a silver, shiny, reflective, metallic hint of a UFO—but no, nothing.

Still, the discourse went on. After a while, the conversation between us went something like this: "Are you prepared to be our voice and talk about us from your perspective—to take the fear out of UFO abductions on our behalf?"

I responded with, "Yes, of course I will." The conversation took the most part of twenty minutes, and a lot more was said. Basically, the outcome was that if I were prepared to lose my job and some of my friends, then they would arrange for me to speak on their behalf. I agreed.

That day went like any other, and I soon forgot about the southbound trip to Bellingen and all that was said. I basically continued my day as if it were like any other (there was nothing I could do), and I certainly didn't discuss it with anyone. I never did.

God knows how, but I was contacted by a Mr. Bill Chalker, who is one of several investigators of UFO phenomenon, sightings, and contact and is a skeptic in the field. He has written many papers, books, and lectures on the subject, but he is still a hard man to convince. (He is very much along the lines of a "Scully," not a "Mulder" in *The X-Files.*)

During our telephone conversation, he advised me he would be in Coffs Harbour on a certain date, and he wished to meet with me. He did meet with me. We discussed a lot about the phenomenon that both he and I had heard about and what I had experienced. He listened to my claims while making non-judgmental responses and unbiased statements. He urged me to fly to Sydney with free accommodation to be a guest on *A Current Affair* with an American expert on UFOs, abductions, and missing time, Mr. Budd Hopkins. He did, however, suggest that to save myself from ridicule or any adverse spin-offs from the appearance, I had every right to ask the camera crew to blank out my face or muffle my voice.

Within a week, I was on my way to Sydney and was taken to the Sebel Townhouse for my overnight stay. The next morning, I was driven to a place in North Sydney. I'm sure it was someone's home, and an area in their lounge was set up with cameras and lights. There was not only camera crew, but also other people there as well, standing around. Quite a crowd had accumulated. I had no idea what they were going to ask me or what I was going to say; there were no scripts or preconceived notions of how this interview was going to go or what it was about, other than UFOs. To my surprise, I was not the only person being interviewed on the show. Budd Hopkins from the USA, who has had a lot of experience and investigative knowledge on ET phenomena, was there. Budd has written many books on the subject and has interviewed thousands of people after claiming they had been abducted, seen ETs, seen UFOs, or had experienced missing time.

Bill urged me to ask the film crew to blank out my face or change my voice so that no one would recognize me, but I felt that if I was coming from truth, no matter how controversial or strange the subject, then I had no reason to hide from the world. I was not embarrassed or ashamed, nor was I about to be made to feel like a fool by anyone.

If I lost friends because of this, then they were not friends, in my opinion. If I lost a job because of this, then so be it. God obviously had a different direction planned for me. I was a firm believer that whatever road we are guided down, no matter how hard or unpleasant, there was a reason for it. *Bring it on,* I thought.

I had no fear of consequences, even though my alien friends had warned me that there might be some type of fall-out or adverse repercussion from this national TV coverage. It did not concern me. What needed to be said—and the thought of them asking me to be their spokesperson—was far more important than any personal effects that may have occurred in my life. That was secondary to the importance of speaking out about a subject that had always been covered, hidden, and shut off to the public. I realized it would be a difficult subject to talk about on national TV without some type of negativity being reflected back upon me. I was in a high-profile, professional type of job as an RN and educator, and I had a lot to lose, but I also had the faith that those who knew me knew I wasn't an idiot or some fly-by-night grandstander. I was a very professional and down-to-earth person who didn't lack intelligence or common sense. My decision was based on trying to relinquish the fear most people felt regarding this subject. It wasn't about me; it was about the subject.

Everything I say about UFOs and aliens, from my perspective, has been the absolute truth. Therefore, I went on TV and was heard and seen openly and honestly. Needless to say, one of my best friends from Sydney didn't speak to me for over a decade, stating that because I had not ever revealed or confided any of this subject matter to her about UFOs or abductions, I had to have been lying. After all, she said, we were good friends, so if I didn't tell her, then it wasn't true, in her opinion. If she felt this way, then this was not the sort of friendship I wanted in my life, so we parted ways.

Within a week, I had lost my job in the private hospital as an ante-natal educator, while a few colleagues sniggered and laughed behind my back. The suspicions of a backlash such as this were practically a prerequisite for the interview, so I was prepared for it, especially with Bill and the ET warning me that the chances were high that this sort of thing could happen. I was okay with the repercussions, because I will never hide the truth or be scared of the consequences from telling it.

While down in Sydney, Bill had arranged for a professional psychologist, Dick Warburton. At that time, he was working at the Sydney University along with several witnesses to take me back in time, through hypnosis, to have the entire event recorded on tape. (The sound track is inaudible, though I still have it.)

Bill drove me to the home of Dick Warburton in Sydney, where he and his wife resided. There were others there watching on. Once again, I had no nervousness or preconceived notions of what was going to be asked. I just relaxed and let whatever was going to happen, happen. I had nothing to hide. I was taken back to my childhood and was aware of everything I spoke about, while seeing everything as if I were actually there in the present time as a small child. It was like I was taken back in time with clarity.

This hypnotism was unbelievable, because I could feel myself going into unchartered areas of memory. Then, all of a sudden, I was in familiar territory again. Remember in a previous chapter when my friend, Pam, hypnotized me? She jumped me forward in twenty-minute increments, whereas this man took me through minute by minute. I felt myself going through unfamiliar ground and then into the areas where Pam had previously taken me. This is how I knew without a doubt that my abductions were real and none of it was imagined or made up. I didn't have the notion or deceitfulness to make this up as I went along, and I most certainly wasn't clued in enough to join all the pieces together. It was all done effortlessly, without thought, thereby joining the old with the new in a seamless explanation, making it so much clearer in my own mind than the disjointed, confusing result of the initial hypnotism. It all matched up, which to me proved its authenticity.

I have no idea how long I was under hypnosis, but I do recall, as the four-year-old child during the abduction, I cried to the point of sobbing relentlessly at the suggestion, "Now you're returning home to your family." I wanted to stay with them. I recall Dick Warburton (the psychologist) floundering because of his lack of background history on my childhood. He was unsure how my home life was and whether I didn't want to return home because of fear or unhappiness. There was no physical or emotional reason why I should not wish to return home to my family. This proved to me that I cared about them a great deal. That shocked me more than a little, because previous to the hypnotism, I had no idea how close I felt to my alien friends. Yet I returned home, to be taken many times in the future. I recognized the little greys, the inside of the ship, the way I got from my bed to the ship, and the external silence (no sounds of engines, no air-conditioning, no voices, just utter silence).

Being back in the ship, I also recognized the internal dialogue (telepathy), the messages sent to me, and the messages I was picking up as I tuned in to their silent conversations. One can eavesdrop. I'm not sure if you're allowed, but I know through experience that you can overhear another's conversation (telepathically), because I've done it. I feel it is very important for my readers to know that even when in utter fear, one must try to stop the inner chatter of your mind, because all that fear and chatter prevents the discourse of conversation from being received. It is this conversation that will give you reasons and explanations and set your mind at rest. They don't just stare blatantly like robots, but are trying hard to communicate. For you to receive this, you must be inwardly and outwardly silent and receptive.

On my return to Coffs Harbour and losing my job, my life continued until, after exhausting all avenues of work in the Coffs Harbour area, I eventually decided on a move up to Queensland with my son. As one door closes, another one is opened. Life is change. We cannot be scared of change, as this is the key to our development, our progress, and our happiness.

Budd Hopkins was amazed how out of all the thousands of people he had interviewed, very few had no fear at all regarding abductions. He said that the entire event was usually a fearful one—but not to me. On that, he felt I was different. My answer to that was that due to the fact that I was taken as a small baby, maybe the frequent abductions gave me a relationship of sorts with them. I didn't feel the fear. But now I believe it was because I have known them for more than one incarnation. It has been ongoing.

In addition, learning and understanding their telepathy (the best, most universal language in the world) gave me a closer relationship than with most, because I was brought up using this silent language with them.

Several weeks after my return to Coffs Harbour, Bill sent me a large envelope with a bunch of papers inside, requesting I fill them in and return them to him so he could use my story in a paper he was writing. He said that when he was writing papers on abductees, he preferred to have mental assessments done to check mental status, authenticity, and honesty. He needed to know that each of his subjects was mentally sound, and it was proven that I was indeed sound and very normal—although I could have told him that.

Chapter Twenty

Coincidences

Coincidences are part of life. Some individuals experience more than others, even on a daily basis. The simple meaning of the word *coincidence* per the Oxford Dictionary is "remarkable concurrence of events, apparently by chance," or in my words, "two incidences, a thought and an action, occurring at the same time." I choose to think that they are not by chance, but by divine intervention; therefore, they must *not* be taken lightly.

Speaking of coincidences, I would like to share with you several of these wonderful experiences or miracles that have taken place in my own life. In my instance, these were telepathic warnings, giving me time to act upon them. These coincidences, to me, are typical of the telepathic messages I have been receiving for most of my life, but each one of these has been a lifesaver. Telepathic messages don't come from thin air, nor do they come from Satan, as some religious bodies infer. They are not imagined in my head as part of a mental illness. They are real, and they are indeed lifesaving occurrences that could be said to be miracles.

I tend to think my capacity to receive these messages is in part the result of the sensitivities or the gifts most abductees are given. I want you to know all human beings have the capacity to receive incoming messages or warnings like these.

1. In 1975, while backpacking around Europe on a six-month journey into countries I had never seen before, I was privy to or the recipient of several lifesaving events. Had I not been sensitive enough to hear or pick up the telepathy, I could have died or been hurt many times over. Sensing telepathy is likened to having a helping hand through the tough times, thereby allowing action to be taken to avoid the consequences of a less-than-perfect outcome.

I was travelling a good part of my journey with an African-American girl, also named Judy. On this particular night, our train had stopped at our destination—San Sebastian, Spain. It was 3:00 a.m., cold, dark, and sprinkling with a fine mist of rain—enough to dampen one's clothes without feeling the rain on one's face.

Neither of us knew where we were going, apart from using the maps we perused on the last leg of our journey on the train. Nothing was open at 3:00 a.m. With map in hand, we decided to walk to the youth hostel in the hope of sleeping on the hostel doorstep or lawn. (Incidentally, we weren't the only ones with that thought.) Instead, we slept on the concrete floor of an underground car park directly across the road from the youth hostel, where it was a little warmer and not so open to the elements.

Judy and I had just stepped off the train, along with several other people who all seemed to disappear into obviously preorganised cars that had met the arriving train, leaving us quite alone on the platform at 3:00 a.m. We decided the safest thing to do was to make our way to the youth hostel, even though we knew we would be knocking on a locked door on our arrival. We felt we would be safer there, in their grounds, than in a train station with no one around. We had previously made a plan of protection by carrying loose pepper in our coat pockets, used by pinching some between our fingers and blowing it into the eyes of an attacker, should the need arise. I had a tail comb at the ready in my hand, while Judy went with a sharpened lead pencil. Neither of these were weapons, but they could be used as such in an emergency.

We decided to shorten the trip by taking a shortcut through the back streets, making our way to the main road, then walking through the city to the other end of town to more smaller streets, finally arriving at the youth hostel in the opposite direction.

We were walking down a dark back street running parallel with the main road, talking about this and that, when on our right was another short street that our map showed us would lead us to the main road. Much to our horror, approaching us and spreading out right across the street, were five young men. They were all drunk and obviously had something sinister in mind to do with us. Between them and us, there was that one side street (our escape) to the right, so I said to Judy, "Whatever you do, don't let them hear what language we are speaking, and get your pepper and your pencil ready."

I also whispered to her that we should continue to walk in the centre of the road at a normal speed, but get ready to run when we reached the small road to the right. Judy became very scared, and my adrenaline started pumping, giving us that "fight or flight" one needs when fear takes hold. We had two things in our favor—we were petrified, and we were not drunk. Therefore, we had speed and alertness on our sides.

As we reached the corner, we turned into the side street. As soon as we got out of sight from the boys, we took off like bullets. We made it to the main road, turning left onto it and running to save our lives. Breathless and sweating, even though it was cold, we took our turn to the left before they made their appearance around the corner. We could hear them yelling out in Spanish. Thank goodness we couldn't understand them.

This is when the telepathy kicked in. I was being intuited to move hastily to the centre of the road, where we would find our escape from danger. I whispered loudly to Judy, who was hot on my heels, "We have to run in the centre of the road. I don't know why, but we have to." The centre of the road was a grassy mid-strip separating the right and left sides of the road. It had high, uninterrupted, wire fencing running the length of the road, seeming to go for miles with thick hedging on either side, that prevented us from crossing the road to get out of sight.

My question was, "Why were we being intuited to go to the centre of the road, when the hedge and wire fence were clearly going to prevent us from escaping?" Oh, ye of little faith. I trusted what was intuited to me, so we continued running breathlessly, with fear giving us wings along the hedged and fenced partition on the centre strip. We heard them break onto the main road, screaming at us from the side street we had just come from. We had managed to lengthen the distance between us.

As I was running, I had my right hand dragging along the hedge, hoping to feel a gap or something I couldn't see in the dark. All of a sudden, while running as fast as anyone could with a backpack on their back, I found one. Stopping abruptly with Judy banging into me, I pulled her through the hedge after me. Not only was there a gap in the hedge, but the fence was also broken enough to easily get through to the other side of the road. We ran through the gap and continued to gain more distance between the boys and us.

Glancing back, we could see them jumping up, trying to see where we were over the hedge. They obviously saw us escape through the hedge, but they couldn't find the same gap. Something miraculous had happened. Luckily for us, they never did find it. Was it made for us to escape? Did it indeed close up after us? Or were they too drunk to find it? We didn't find our answer out until our return back to the train station the following day. We eventually found our way to the youth hostel, but due to the drizzly weather, a sheltered area across the road from the youth hostel in an underground parking area of a block of flats gave us far more comfort than a wet, cold lawn.

There were over a dozen people on the lawns of the hostel with the same dilemma as us (arriving too late to get in). Scattered across the lawns were pitched pup-tents and people sprawled on the lawns. Our decision to sleep in the car park was a much better one than the wet lawn.

The following day, returning to the train station, we walked the length of that road along the hedge in the centre of the road, deliberately searching for the gap in the hedge. There were no breaks in that fence or hedge to be found, and we were looking hard for them. It was an intuited escape route made for us, and I believe it was closed after we made our way through the gap to prevent the boys from following us. The boys never found it, and I know they were looking for it, because they would have seen us escape through it. My belief was that it had closed over miraculously, saving our lives. The intuited message did say that we would find our escape, so to me, it was a planned event especially for us.

2. In the early 1980s, while returning to my home in Dee Why, I was driving down a rather steep incline on a main road in North Sydney when I heard that familiar telepathy out of the blue. I was instructed to pull in at the petrol station at the bottom of the hill to get my left rear inner tyre checked. As far as I was concerned, there was nothing wrong with my car, its tyres, or its wheels at all.

There were no noises, no pulling to the left or right, no wobbling, or no hint that anything was wrong. But as usual, I do listen to these warnings. As I reached the bottom of the hill, I put my indicator on and followed the instruction to turn into the petrol station at the bottom of the hill on the corner to the left.

Being a mere female, I had no idea what to look for. I approached one of the men in the workshop wearing an overall. I urged him to come with me to take a look at my tyre. The man lay on his back in his grease-stained overalls and pulled himself under the car. He took his time and finally slid out from underneath my car, asking me curiously, "What made you feel you had to get your tyre checked, if you felt no changes in your car's handling?"

I replied, "You wouldn't believe me if I told you."

He then made my hair stand on end with his discourse. "Lady, if you would have driven another mile, you would have had a blowout—a terrible accident. This tyre has fibres fraying out of it, and it's red-hot and bulging. The reason you didn't feel it was because it was on the inside of the tyre and not the usual place on the tread. It was about to explode. My God, you are lucky." He then asked me again, "So tell me, what made you come in to get it checked, if you didn't know anything was wrong?"

"Just a feeling," I said with a knowing smile. We immediately pushed it into the workshop and got a new tyre put on. Once again, I was saved by listening to that telepathic lifesaving message from who-knows-where.

3. Bellingen was another place where someone out there stepped in to save my life. This one will definitely send shivers down your spine, because it did mine. I was driving home from my job as a nurse at the Bellingen Chemist Shop in the early 1990s and was approaching a slightly winding, steep uphill climb with an overtaking lane. The oncoming lane was for single-lane traffic only, coming down the hill. Seeing as it was only a short overtaking lane and there was no traffic at all in either direction, I felt it wouldn't hurt to stay in the overtaking lane. I would have moved into it anyway as I neared its end at the top of the hill, so I remained there for my upward climb with no sign of any cares in either direction.

I was driving up the hill when that wonderful intuited message began, "Get over into the left-hand lane *now!*" I checked my rear vision mirror, and the road in both directions was clear. There were no cars at all, so I second-guessed the intuition and remained where I was on the overtaking lane near the middle of the road, ignoring the warning. The message came again, this time very plainly: "Move into your left lane now—*now!*"

This sounded urgent, so once again, I checked my rear-vision mirror and side mirror and looked at the oncoming lane. There was not a car on the road but my own, but due to the urgency of the repeated message, I indicated and slowly moved into the left lane. As I was moving over, a star wagon appeared, coming over the hill in an oncoming direction, safely in its own lane. Suddenly and without warning, its front right tyre exploded.

Everything from that point onward appeared to be in slow motion. Thank goodness there were no other cars on the road. The van rolled over and over as the front right tyre blew out. It seemed to roll diagonally over and over again, until it slid. It scraped screeched, and made shrill noises as the metal scraped across the bitumen, finally coming to a halt on my side of the road. Glass and parts of the car were flying through the air slowly and landing on the ground with a bounce, leaving the ground again and twisting through the air. Finally, the parts came to rest all over the road.

Should I have remained in the lane where I was, I would have been completely wiped out. I was definitely in his line of fire. He missed me by a matter of centimeters as I was making my way over. Still no cars appeared on the road, and a complete silence reigned as everything stopped.

I pulled my car to a halt on the ash, felt at the side of the road, and yanked on my brake. I turned the engine off and opened the boot, taking out a huge fishing tackle box (my first aid kit). I ran to the star wagon, and as a nurse, I just did what I was trained to do. I yelled out, asking if everyone was okay, and then asked how many people were in the vehicle. The driver's door was the only door that could open, but due to the car's rolling, it ended up on its side, so the door was facing upward. I scaled up to the top of the car and helped the driver open the door, pulling it open like a trap door.

As I pulled each child up and out of the door, the driver, the father of the children, was getting them from their seats and pushing them up toward me. His wife was helped out after the last child made its exit. I asked him to hand me any blankets or pillows from the van, using those as a soft place for his family to sit. I sat all three children and his wife on the side of the road against the guard rail and dressed their wounds. The husband was hurt the worst. The adrenaline that had enabled him to help push everyone out was starting to wane. He became a little dizzy, even though he still felt no pain.

He remained in the van at this time, because I couldn't pull him out, and his energy was insufficient to pull himself out using his injured arm (incidentally, he had no muscle on his forearm). The next vehicle to come over the hill top was a big truck. I managed to wave him down. The driver was very helpful and courteous. He had a CB radio (this was in the days before mobile phones), and he called an ambulance and assisted me in pulling the father out of the van. His arm was scraped to the bone; it was a mess. It was amazing how he was able to do so much with it before we noticed how bad it was. He was in far worse shape than any other member of his family. The truck driver helped with traffic control and started waving the traffic around the crashed vehicle while halting the cars in the opposite direction. He did a great job. What amazed me was that during the entire incident, not one car appeared on the road in either direction. This was a major arterial road on the highway. Once the accident was over, cars appeared and started piling up in both directions—amazing. Everyone lived to tell the tale, but I'm afraid if I hadn't have moved over into the left lane when I very plainly heard the warning, it could very possibly have been a whole different story—one of tragedy. With the telepathic warning, I was able to avoid a head-on collision.

When the ambulance arrived, I gave a hand-over of events for each patient, got into my intact car, and drove home, giving thanks for such an effective warning from my invisible friends. This only goes to show that we are constantly being observed and helped if we believe what we hear and take heed.

4. While living in Auckland, New Zealand, my girlfriend Liz Howe and myself were returning home following an evening's outing together downtown. We hadn't been drinking, being only seventeen years old and therefore unable to even get into the bars or pubs. In those days, the drinking age was twenty-one years old. While making our way home on the motorway, I had a telepathic intuit which felt like an overwhelming urge to flick my headlights off and on. This flicking of lights seemed ludicrous to me, yet I was compelled to continue, as if there was a real reason behind the apparent childishness. It was not something I would normally do.

Even though it puzzled me as to why I was actually doing this, I continued, passing the car in front, then dropping back behind them, flicking my headlights up on full beam and passing them again. I was in front of the car when suddenly, my engine coughed and spluttered and just gave up the ghost. I dropped behind them as the car overtook me and had to pull over on the side of the road. The car stopped and couldn't be started again. It was then that I noticed my petrol light on. I'd run out of petrol.

Liz and I just sat there, wondering what on earth we were going to do, especially if this person in the car I'd been annoying stopped too. Then it hit me that I was being intuited to do this to get the other car to stop, because we had run out of petrol in the middle of a dark highway with no help or phone boxes for miles.

The car that was now in front of us pulled up and reversed back toward us. I was really concerned that he might punch us or get angry at our behavior on the right. A man alighted, walking back toward our car. I was envisaging an awful scene because of my behavior— what appeared to be playfully flicking my headlights on and off at him. He arrived at my window and knocked. I wound down my window to an angry voice, asking, "What the hell do you two think you are doing playing on the motorway like that, flicking your lights up and down? Do have any idea how dangerous that is? Well? What have you got to say for yourselves?"

I looked him straight in the eye and said, "Thank God you stopped. I had been trying to attract your attention, because I was nearly out of petrol, and now we are in the middle of nowhere with no way of getting help—and here you stopped. Thank you so much." The mood very rapidly turned. He smiled, said he was sorry, and offered to take us to a petrol station to get some petrol. The story ended perfectly with this angry man turning into a good Samaritan and driving us to a petrol station to bring some petrol back to our crippled car. This started out as a seemingly silly game. I had no idea how it was going to play out, but it ended up being a lifesaving event. The flicking of lights was our saving grace, and it wasn't until the car stopped that I realized how miraculous this really was. Someone else knew the reason this played out before I did. I certainly was not the type of person to play any games on the road. All my life, I had been a responsible girl and didn't get any joy from playing dangerous road games—or anything dangerous, for that matter. Little did I know there was a reason behind it. I didn't click onto it until the car had stopped.

5. In 2010 and 2011 at Christmas time, amongst the Queensland pouring rains and pursuing floods that destroyed thousands of homes evacuated many more, I was studiously sitting at my desk, editing

this book. My computer is a new Apple, and I am thrilled with it, but something strange was happening. I would do hours of editing, accomplishing a lot of ground, and when I went to save those changes, they didn't happen. I was doing the work and losing it.

In frustration, while trying to get the "save" prompt to work, I experienced an intuited message. It was to change the channel on the television to SBS and watch what was on. I had no idea what was on, and this was a channel I had never watched before. I did not even know what number I had to press to get it. Mid-sentence with my editing, I scrambled through the TV times to find what number I had to press to get a channel I'd never watched before. I knew whatever I had to watch was important, but I had no clue what it was.

A psychiatrist would no doubt have me diagnosed as being a schizophrenic (hearing voices), but I want to reassure you that I was not hearing voices. I just had an intuited thought to do something I normally wouldn't have any inclination of doing. I got up to do just that. I am sensitive enough in the telepathy department to know when I'm getting an incoming message and have common sense enough to know what is dangerous or wrong and what is innocent or harmless. To my way of thinking, changing the television channel was harmless. It still seemed important, so I got up and found the television program.

At last, I found the paper and worked out that I had to press thirty-one on my television remote control to actually get SBS. I had never watched this channel before. There, to my utter amazement, was a documentary playing. It was called My Mother Talks to Aliens. It was about a woman named Mary Rodwell and her efforts to get this subject out there in the world and recognized as a phenomenon, a reality, and not a belief system. She was also trying to take the fear out of abduction, the same as myself. Mary actually invited debates with scientists and scholars—which, in my opinion, is futile, as scientists believe that if you can't see it, test it, or feel it, then it's not real and doesn't exist. It's a shame that brilliant scholars are so closed-minded.

The coincidence (in my life, they are daily occurrences) of actually seeing on screen exactly what I was writing about was once again fantastically and amazingly coincidental. This alone is evidence that telepathy is real. I can't pick something like that out of thin air. This was definitely a message sent to me to either confirm what I was writing about or tell me this was a lady I had to contact to work with. Was I actually being given a contact? What followed, in fact, was a series of contacts. Following the end of the documentary, I found Mary's e-mail address on her web site and wrote to her immediately. Within a very short time, I received a response. We e-mailed back and forth until I phoned her. We had a long and interesting conversation. She, in turn, has given me three more contacts—and this is how life works.

My background training as a registered nurse, educator, and counsellor had me asking her to put me on her list of practitioners to professionally see people who had been abducted and might be keeping this to themselves—people who were fighting to suppress the images or pictures playing out in their minds. Not only was I trained to help individuals as a counsellor, but I also had experienced these visions and feelings all through my life. Now it was time to put my training to good use and pay it forward for humanity.

There are many more coincidences and intuited messages I have experienced, but this will suffice thus far. Expect another book when I actually have a successful meeting and get answers to many of the questions we crave answers for.

Conclusion

I was born a normal, healthy, female child weighing six pounds, twelve ounces. I was breastfed for nine months, and I suddenly ended up in hospital with pylonephritis, during which time my first of many abductions began. I went through life ignorant of the abductions, knowing at the time that all was well, but was returned void of any contact whatsoever. I was the recipient of wondrous gifts, unlike most children. Even I didn't recognize myself as being any different from anyone else. It's strange how we choose to keep our secret thoughts to ourselves while realizing others don't think the same way. I was basically average with my studies, never coming in at the bottom, while never really coming in at the top of anything, either—except for physical education (namely, swimming), athletics, and gymnastics. In sports, I got to receive the winner's first prize cup on an annual basis.

My attendance records during my school and employment years were exemplary. I never had a sick day at school, and upon leaving school, I was the only nurse in my group who didn't have to make time up at the end of my training. A knowledge that I was in control of all my hopes and dreams for my future was built into my psyche. I knew I could do or be whatever I wanted, with good, hard work and application. Yes, there were knock-backs, but success was mine, if that was what I wanted. This goes for everyone, not just me. My entire life was a means of working my way through every job and course I ever wanted, equipping myself with knowledge to help others while enjoying the journey, and striving for my goals.

From infancy right through to present time, I was abducted by small individuals from another world. As a child, I know I was tested, sampled, and educated. This education was not on the school syllabus, but more so on attitudes like empathy, compassion, love, caring, kindness, generosity, sharing, planetary history, the structure and function of craft, ideas for the future, and many other topics.

Much of what the aliens do to us remains a puzzle to me because of the usual amnesia we each have inflicted upon us on our return, making us believe we haven't been anywhere but in our beds, sleeping all night. Often times there are hints of strange things, like bruises, blood stains on pillows or skin, and strange marks. The amnesia we are given is not only a means of protecting them and their plight, but us as well. A genetic change takes place to prevent damage to the body and mind, and this protects us during the transition from bed to space and back again. Quite often, a side effect is amnesia. In between all the chapters of my life, approximately every second year, the abductions continued with no interference to my life whatsoever.

My desires and goals were to heal, help, and save the world and everybody in it in as many areas as I could. This has been my goal from childhood and still is to this day.

I still continue to study—to cram into my mind everything that excites me and that I am enthusiastic about. It is a joy, a challenge, and a goal. What we cram into our minds is, in part, the only baggage we can take with us when we leave this earth. My life is being crammed with whatever I can learn. I wanted to leave my mark as someone who truly cared about humanity and would step out on a limb to do so. Thus far, I would like to think I've saved many lives in one way or another. This desire began when I was a child—around the time of my four-year-old abduction. The feelings of compassion are soul-deep.

My heart and dreams are in giving to the human race, and I feel combined with our aliens. This is the usual plight of most abductees— to help others and be an example of goodness. Was my life run by myself, or did my open prayer on the road to Howick back in 1972, where I swore to give myself in service to God and humanity, take effect from that point onward? I think so. I asked to be guided, and I believe I have been all my life.

I often ask myself, "If abductions or aliens are thought of as evil or harmful, why is it that most abductees turn out to be gentle, kind, compassionate, caring, creative, and artistic human beings who go out of their way to help people? And how come we are all returned?" In my opinion, this is not evil.

My strong desire to help third-world countries and those struck down by wars, natural disasters, and catastrophes had me applying to Care Australia, Red Cross, World Vision, and any aid service I can find to donate my services. Guess what? Not one of them even gave me the courtesy of a response—nothing. It seemed all they wanted was money. I was prepared to give up my work, life, home, and family for humanity, and I was ignored. This happened in 1972 when Saigon was taken over and has happened during all the tsunamis, earthquakes, wars, and catastrophes worldwide that have happened ever since, right up to the floods in Queensland in December 2010.

All the rejections by these good-will companies didn't prevent me from continually adding to my repertoire of subjects that I chose to study. I needed to be prepared for every emergency, covering mind, body, and spirit. Having glimmers of recall did answer a lot of questions for me. Feelings I had experienced at differing times in my life only went to make me feel that I was never alone. That is a very reassuring feeling, not a scary one, especially when I know that harm was the last thing they wanted to inflict upon me. If that were so, I would never have been returned from the numerous visits I have had with them. Some people have these snippets of recall that sadly only go to make them feel scared, paranoid, and fearful at night while having many other emotions and associated complaints.

Where this is concerned, a lot of psychiatrists and counsellors without an understanding of this type of phenomenon would automatically classify a person such as an abductee as a schizoid personality (one who hears voices) or a person with some type of psychiatric disorder requiring medications to suppress further so-called imaginings. Perhaps this is why people won't or don't come forward—for fear of being labelled a psychiatric case. They are mostly drugged with antidepressants, sedatives, and relaxants, while never really coming to terms with their inner turmoil. This is where Mary helps a lot of people. Mary is the lady I met from the television program I was intuited to watch. She takes people back to the memories that have been suppressed to help them through their dilemmas.

In reality, these individuals are normal, everyday people with a buried subconscious vision of something frightening happening to them—in human terms, something that is not acceptable. While suppressing feelings and creating phobias, fears, and nightmares and all manner of other problems, many abductees think they are imagining things or develop worse problems trying to cover these memories. They may go into complete denial. However, to release these feelings to someone who knows, cares, and understands specifically about this subject may be just what the doctor ordered, so to speak.

For those of you who have had extraterrestrial or alien meetings or abduction experiences and need to speak to someone who fully understands this type of subconscious effect, just know that you are not sick, crazy, or imagining things, nor are you alone. The truth will always reveal itself. Search the Internet to find places and people that are there for you. Just look up "UFO organizations," and there will be a huge choice of contacts.

An ideal way to unravel the confusing feelings of an abduction is to try a series of treatments with a reputable hypnotist. This allows you to reach beneath the conscious thought into the subconscious mind, where those memories live. Once you reach the reality of what actually happened, quite often, all external symptoms can disappear. If you have any knowledge of hypnotism, it can be very freeing.

During the writing of this book, I had me a very similar feeling. It took me back to the place I was writing about with such wonderful clarity, it's as if I have revisited the experience again, but now have the choice of going in deeper and recalling more of my initial sense of the place through hearing, seeing, smelling, and touching, regardless of distance and time. The mind is more powerful that anyone gives it credit.

We as human beings are very fragile individuals, and we put in place protective mechanisms to prevent ongoing emotional pain. This can happen with everyday traumatic events as well, not only ET involvements. These events can be rape, road accidents, bashings, fires, near-drownings, sharks, wars, and anything accidental or incidental that causes us to change in everyday behavior. It's this emotion that can be locked away, but once released, it can help the situation.

Humanity has spent billions of dollars trying to scan the night sky in an effort to prove whether life exists outside our own world. How ignorant to think humans are the only life source in the universe. Extraterrestrials are more advanced than we are; therefore, when and if they want to be seen, they will reveal themselves—in their time, not ours. The only spacecrafts and aliens we have ever examined are those that have accidentally crashed, which proves they are around. But our governments have tried to protect us in keeping it from us—or is it themselves they are trying to protect? When our alien friends decide the time is right to communicate with us, it will be done. Until then, they will be our elusive friends that come into our galaxy to observe us and fulfill their part of the contract in doing whatever it is they are doing. We must know and realize it is not to destroy us, because they would have done it by now. It makes sense they wouldn't travel from the ends of the earth to attack us for no reason.

Keep mindful there are many planets and many different species of aliens, all with different appearances, attitudes, intentions, and intelligences. I cannot speak for all alien nations, but from the years I have been with the greys, I feel I can safely vouch for their priority in saving our planet, regardless of what they are doing to us, for us, and with us. We are the race that is destroying the planet we live on, and we are the ones who dig out Earth's core; draining it of its buffer (oil); stripping it of all its riches, elements, minerals, and resources—all in the name of greed. We have successfully raped our own planet. How can a sphere remain a sphere that is round and magnetically sound when the very guts of it have being stripped out? As we empty

Earth's core, she can't do anything but readjust her centre, resulting in earthquakes in an effort to maintain equilibrium, which in turn affects weather and tidal changes, melting poles, etc. It all starts and ends with humankind itself, and we are showing ourselves to be unworthy of being entrusted with Earth's care.

All I pray is that when they do land to communicate with us, several of their abductees are there to meet and greet them and understand their telepathy enough to interpret what they wish to convey to us. An interpreter needs to be present to relay what they want to say to us, because they can readily pick up what we are thinking. When the day comes that they actually meet us face-to-face—and I believe that day is not far away—we have to accept them gracefully and in friendship and peace, instead of in defense and aggression with barbs and prickles, rules, and regulations, as our human race tends to do, being the aggressive animals we are. When that time comes, it will take some exceptional communication skills. Let there be no more lies, deceit, or propaganda. We have been putting up with those for far too long. I will conclude with some questions to ponder. What will the end of the Mayan calendar in 2012 bring? Will it bring a set of natural disasters? Will there be an increase in spiritual understanding or the union between civilizations from earth and beyond?

A Prayer

I pray that each and every person who reads this book will recognize his or her own truth that dwells within. Recognition of truth will let itself be known and set you free.

I pray that every soul within and without our world is working to join together in peace, love, unity, and progress for the good of all.

I pray that you resist the temptation to give fear power to manifest, as fear is simply a word. Only you have the ability to feed it power—resist.

I pray that each human being on this planet strives to love himself or herself with all his or her heart, mind, and soul. I pray that each loves their neighbors as he or she love himself or herself.

I pray that each and every one of you values your life, regardless of outside influences or personal appearances. May all eyes, ears, and hearts open to receive the love that God sends to you through everyone you meet. Your teachers are those you meet every day, and every outcome has the potential for good. Be mindful of your choices—choose well.

And finally, I pray that our beautiful planet we call Earth exists eternally in the universe, whole, complete, and plentiful in peace, love, and harmony, forever and ever. Amen.